DATE DUE

DEC 00			
NO2 00			
JE 7 03			

DEMCO 38-296

"to do & to be"

Gertrude Barnum / 1866–1948

Mary Dreier / 1876–1963

Pauline Newman / c. 1888–1986

Rose Pesotta / 1896–1965

"to do & to be"

by Ann Schofield

Portraits of Four Women Activists, 1893–1986

Northeastern University Press / Boston

Northeastern University Press

Copyright 1997 by Ann Schofield

Library of Congress Cataloging-in-Publication Data

Schofield, Ann.
To do & to be : portraits of four women activists, 1893–1986 / Ann Schofield.
p.   cm.
Includes index.
ISBN 1–55553–294–2 (cloth).—
ISBN 1–55553–293–4 (pbk.)
1. Women in trade-unions—United States—Biography.   2. Women labor leaders—United States—Biography.   3. Women in labor movement—United States—Biography.   I. Title.
HD6079.2.U5S36   1997
338.4'7'092273—dc20
[B]   96–32143

Designed by Christopher Kuntze

Printed and bound by Thomson-Shore, Inc., in Dexter, Michigan. The paper is Glatfelter Supple Opaque Recycled, an acid-free sheet.

MANUFACTURED IN THE UNITED STATES OF AMERICA
01 00 99 98 97   5 4 3 2 1

FOR

MY PARENTS

Mary Brennan Schofield

and

Patrick Joseph Schofield

AND

IN LOVING MEMORY OF MY BROTHER

Kenneth Schofield

(1950–1980)

CONTENTS

ACKNOWLEDGMENTS

It is a great joy to thank in a more formal way those who have contributed their expertise, hospitality, and support during the years when this book was gestating. Beginning at Binghamton University, my interest in American labor and women and in the questions I explore here was first kindled and sustained under the expert tutelage of Melvyn Dubofsky and Sarah Elbert. As teachers and mentors they offered models of the engaged scholar.

I am grateful for the skillful assistance of librarians and archivists at a long list of institutions: the Walter Reuther Archives at Wayne State University; the Oral History Collection at Columbia University; the Tamiment Institute and Fales Collection of New York University; the New York Public Library; the archives of the International Ladies' Garment Workers' Union and the Amalgamated Clothing Workers of America at the Martin P. Catherwood Library, Cornell University; the Hull House Archives, University of Illinois, Chicago Circle; the Wisconsin State Historical Society; and the International Institute of Social History in Amsterdam. Most especially, though, I would like to thank the staff of the Arthur and Elizabeth Schlesinger Library. Eva Mosley, the late Patricia King, and Diane Hamer offered interest and support during my many visits to that special shrine of women's history.

As notes became drafts and drafts became chapters, I began to take my emerging book "on the road," acquiring another delightful kind of debt. For the generous hospitality of friends and institutions, I thank the Center for Industrial and Labor Relations and the Department of History at the University of California at Berkeley, the History Department of Barnard College, the Trade Union Program and Women's Studies Program of Harvard University, and the Hall Center for the Humanities at the University of Kansas. Nina Asher, Jeffrey Steinberg, Beth Bailey, David Farber, and Deborah Valenze made my frequent New York sojourns "scholar's holidays." And when my manuscript as a collection of diskettes made its way across the Atlantic, Catherine Collomp, Haskell Springer, Anne Fowler, and especially Richard Jenkyns provided kindness, computer advice, and refuge as the book took its final form.

The wisdom of friends and colleagues, generously given, appears on almost every page of this book. For putting aside their own work and reading mine, I thank Eileen Boris, David Brody, Blanche Wiesen Cook, David Katzman, Angel Kwolek-Folland, Elisabeth Israels Perry, Jill Quadagno, Tony Rosenthal, Elizabeth Schultz, Janet Sharistanian, Deborah Valenze, and Nancy Woloch, and members of the Economic and Social History Seminar at the University of Kansas.

My greatest thanks go to four dear friends who read every word of this manuscript more than once. Their trenchant yet kindly given criticism always improved the book; their good cheer encouraged me when my belief in the project lagged. Elizabeth Kuznesof, a splendid scholar and critic, took me in hand when I arrived in Kansas in 1979. Over the years she has been a mentor, a colleague, and a friend. Everything I have written has benefited from her keen insights and editorial skills.

George Cotkin, with so little time to spare, always found some when I needed his vast knowledge and his sharp editor's pen. Our many conversations have continually expanded my sense of the larger philosophical issues that frame my work.

I met Beth Bailey and David Farber when this book was at its midpoint. They made my New York "summer camp" possible, offered me bed and board, and helped me more than anyone else to understand the value of narrative, how to "tell my story."

Scholars, of course, do not live by roses alone. For bread in the form of fellowships and grants, I thank the National Endowment for the Humanities, the General Research Fund of the University of Kansas, two sabbatical leaves from the University of Kansas, the Hall Center for the Humanities, the Kaiser Fund of the Walter Reuther Archives of Wayne State University, and the Radcliffe Scholars Fund.

Sylvia Stone, Pam Levitt, and Pam LeRow were tireless in their support for the production of this manuscript, typing, copying, and mailing many drafts as its author continued her footloose wanderings. My editor, John Weingartner, never waivered in his support of my project since our first meeting over lunch on a spring day in Boston.

The sketch of Gertrude Barnum was done by Sylvia Stone. The photo of Mary Dreier is courtesy of the Arthur and Elizabeth Schlesinger Library, Radcliffe College. The photographs of Pauline Newman and Rose Pesotta were provided courtesy of the Martin P. Catherwood Library, Cornell University.

My book is dedicated to my family. All three believed its author could do anything she set her mind to. And although it has taken some time, perhaps she has.

"to do & to be"

INTRODUCTION

In 1912, reformer Gertrude Barnum published "The Pig-Headed Girl" in the union newspaper, the *Ladies' Garment Worker*. In this short story, Barnum's spunky heroine refused to accept conventional drudgery in her parent's home or in a factory while she awaited marriage and a home of her own. Instead she broke from tradition and enjoyed a freer life. Demanding that her work be meaningful and challenging, she asked, "Why should I accept work men wouldn't take?" She joined a union and, usurping a male prerogative, invented a new process to be used in her trade, exclaiming, "Why should men do all the inventing?" She changed jobs—"Why not a 'rising young woman' as well as a rising young man?" She eventually married a man of her choice and directed the education of her several children rather than having it "dictated by Uncle Methuselah." The pigheaded girl resolutely marched toward her goals impelled by a self-interest antithetical to nineteenth-century notions of womanhood. And her independence enhanced her marital choices rather than making her less suited to marriage.[1]

Barnum's image of the pigheaded girl was a hopeful and feminist vision of the meaning of wage work for women. In her simple tale she confronted one of the most troubling issues of the industrial age—wage work for women. In so doing she accepted its inevitability, acknowledged its positive potential, and, most important for her readers, portrayed work as enhancing rather than precluding maternity.

Less than a year before Barnum's story appeared, however, Americans had confronted an alternative and infinitely more horrific image of the working woman. "The floods of water from the fireman's hose that ran into the gutter were actually stained red with blood," wrote an anguished reporter as he described the tragedy of the Triangle Shirtwaist fire. On March 25, 1911, in New York City, 146 workers, primarily young immigrant women, were killed in a gruesome factory fire.[2]

The Triangle Shirtwaist Company, unfortunately a typical establishment, was located on the seventh, eighth, and ninth floors of a Lower East Side tenement. Low wages and long hours were the norm for the mainly immigrant female workforce. Toilets and the elevator were often broken, drinking water was dirty, and the spark that began the fire easily ignited cartons of flammable fabric in the crowded workroom. A locked door forced terrified workers to escape the inferno by jumping from the window. Newspaper photographs and sketches of their "burned, smashed, soaked" bodies accompanied by outraged editorials showed middle-class Americans a reality long known to reformers and to the city's poor—the urban sweatshop.

In this book I will introduce four women—Gertrude Barnum (1866–1948), Mary Dreier (1876–1963), Pauline Newman (c. 1888–1986), and Rose Pesotta (1896–1965)—who tried to chart the distance between these dramatically different conceptions of the meaning of the industrial age for women. Between 1893 and 1986, these four activists fought to improve the working conditions cast into such grim relief by the Triangle fire and to realize the expansive potential of the pigheaded girl fable. By the end of their lives, they and activists like them felt confident that they had eliminated the sweatshop and had brought dignity into the working world of women, particularly immigrants in America's huge mass-production apparel industry.

This book tells the story of these four women's work in the various movements—settlement, suffrage, feminist, and trade union—that acknowledged the centrality of wage work to women's lives in the twentieth century. The political labels they wore—feminist, socialist, anarchist, or liberal—all identified an idealistic commitment to social change. The strategies they employed—consumer education, protective legislation, and union organization—contributed to the welfare policies and institutions created in the United States during the 1930s. And the stories that they themselves told about women, work, and their own lives constructed narratives with new insights into the nature of femininity and the role of women in modern America.

Hundreds of women enlisted in the cause of labor during the late nineteenth century and throughout the twentieth. Why do these four merit our attention? First, each in her own way was an important agent in changing the status of women workers, particularly in the garment trades. Barnum began her activist career at Jane Addams's Hull House and went on to organize and write for the International Ladies' Garment Workers' Union (ILGWU). Dreier was a suffragist and cofounder of the New York Women's Trade Union League (NYWTUL). Newman, who immigrated at an early age, was a factory worker, a firebrand socialist organizer, and then a union official. Pesotta, also an immigrant, began and ended her working life in garment factories but during the 1930s and 1940s was the highest-ranked woman unionist in America. All four individuals organized women into unions, investigated factory conditions, promoted regulatory legislation, forged links, often tenuous, between women of different classes, and confronted the sexual politics of work, which included discrimination in unions and sexual harassment on the shop floor. In a prescient fashion they expressed concern for the welfare of women in the workplace and outside it as well.

Second, the biographies of these four women offer us the history of women and labor from a perspective rarely seen. Neither generals nor foot soldiers in the struggle to create a more just and equitable world for women workers, they were like commanders in the field, popularizing and deploying ideas and strategies. While Barnum, Dreier, Newman, and Pesotta did not create the material and conceptual universe in which they lived, which conditioned their understanding, they spoke in their writings and speeches, and in their own activist lives, of the possibilities that they hoped modernity offered women. As social reformers they implicitly did cultural work by creating new models of womanhood that incorporated wage labor into the female life cycle.

The efforts of these four women to create images of themselves and of femininity led each of them to produce a wide array of narratives—memoirs, novels, short stories, and autobiographies. Some of these documents found publishers and readers; others remain in handwritten or typescript form in archival boxes. Such narratives offered their authors controlled spheres within which the ambivalence of modernity could be figured and resolved. The narratives offer us the possibility of seeing these women's utopian visions. The "Pig-Headed Girl," for example, found fulfillment in both wage work and domesticity. Neither sexual harassment nor unsanitary work conditions threatened her virtue or her fitness for motherhood; neither conflict with her family nor the restrictive demands of gender marred her sense of accomplishment.

The narratives also give us a clearer notion of how the four women presented themselves. None of my subjects lived in a conventional household or had a traditional marriage. None was biologically a mother. Yet most chose the language and the narrative form of romance to mediate critical issues related to women and work. When writing about their own lives, Newman and Pesotta's narratives followed patterns used by other Jewish immigrants.

In the following chapters, I have arranged the four biographies like a string quartet: each introduces a particular theme, which is then amplified or modified by the next. Barnum strikes themes of the settlement experience, relations between native-born and immigrant women, mediation between capital and labor, and suffrage as a reform strategy. Dreier's life presents variations on these themes and adds government activity, feminist organizations, and the "Boston marriage." The stories of Pauline Newman and Rose Pesotta, both immigrants, highlight the importance and the contradictions of leftist politics for politicized women and, in the case of Pesotta, the particular challenges of organizing women workers during the 1930s and 1940s.

The careers of these women do more than illustrate the significant milestones in the labor and women's movements in U.S. history. By exploring their personal lives as well as their public ones, we introduce a subjective element into history. Through biography we may ask—and try to learn—how individuals come to accept ideas, to act on them, and to change. Precisely this subjectivity, a response at the point where the individual and history intersect, is a central concern of the present book.

The subjectivity that characterizes biography must of course be situated. The emotions, sensibilities, and political thought that set these individuals apart cannot be understood without placing them in their social and historical context. Between 1893, when Gertrude Barnum first came to Hull House, and 1986, when Pauline Newman died, American history spanned events with global ramifications—two world wars, the Great Depression, the turmoil of the 1960s. The domestic face of America changed as well during those years. By the turn of the century, business, finance, commercial agriculture, and skilled labor were well on their way to organization on a national scale and more and more understood the usefulness of Washington. In fact, during the twentieth century, the state came to play an ever larger role in the lives of individuals and social institutions in America.

Immigrants transformed the population during the last decade of the nineteenth century and the years preceding the First World War. Millions of Europeans and Asians flooded into the United States to feed the nation's voracious hunger for labor. Densely populated urban neighborhoods in New York, Chicago, Boston, and other American cities became polyglot crucibles where traditional cultures encountered industrial life.

In the late nineteenth century, as my subjects stepped onto the public stage, social signposts of modernity appeared in forms that included not only increased numbers of wage-earning women but also a declining birthrate, access to higher education for elite women, and a rejuvenated women's movement. Historians agree that immigrant, native-born, rural, urban, black, white, middle-class, and working-class women were *all* affected by the stupendous changes wrought by industrialization. Did women belong in public life? The topic of gender, or in the words of the time, "the woman question," became the subject of debate. Barnum, Dreier, Newman, and Pesotta made strikingly different life choices that can fruitfully be examined in the context of the work, ideologies, organizations, and sexuality that formed the framework of their lives.

WORK

Wage labor most obviously gave women an increasingly public role in the modern world. But work also illustrated the way in which the cost and benefit of social change fell differentially upon women. Wage work meant one thing for middle-class women and something dramatically different for working-class, often immigrant, women. Simply put, work liberated middle-class women from the social constraints of marriage, while the work done out of necessity by poor women was almost always oppressive. The millions of immigrant women from southern and Eastern Europe who flooded into the United States in the late nineteenth century encountered modernity in sweatshops, domestic service, and garment factories. Most were eager to flee these jobs for marriage.

Women's seemingly traditional choice, however, was often modified by their New World experiences.[3] In contrast to their mothers, who defined themselves by their family roles, these women had an additional role that structured consciousness and identity. Writing of an Italian garment worker in 1919 whose first English words were "feenisher" "dress" or "cloding," reformer Louise Odencrantz commented that "her work often forms the strongest link with her new world."[4]

Industrial work shaped exceptional immigrant women like Pauline Newman and Rose Pesotta just as it did Odencrantz's anonymous finisher. Their firsthand experience of sweatshop life with its hazards and insecurities persuaded them as nothing else could of the need for industrial reform. They left the shops, though, not, as most women did, for traditional marriages but rather for careers in the International Ladies' Garment Workers' Union. Their careers as organizers and as union officials afforded them the same opportunity available to women from more elite backgrounds. Their work provided them with income and a platform for their political views while also enabling them to structure their personal and intimate lives in ways other than by marrying. In other words, work gave them an independence unusual for women even in early twentieth-century America.

Modernity meant work also for middle-class women born in the United States at this time. Medicine, librarianship, and academic life all attracted female pioneers in the late nineteenth and early twentieth century.[5] Women like Gertrude Barnum and Mary Dreier, who shared the concerns of Newman, Pesotta, and others regarding social justice and women workers, gravitated toward settlement houses and reform organizations. Urban settlements, located in the very impoverished immigrant communities they served, narrowed the distance between middle- and working-class women. But they also offered educated women like Gertrude Barnum a community of like-minded intellectuals, a legitimate profession, and the spiritual rewards of commitment to a noble cause.[6] While settlement houses were the best-known and arguably the most unusual reform organizations, they were not the only such communities. Reform organizations like the cross-class Women's Trade Union League (WTUL) provided equivalent benefits of community and purpose for other elite women like Mary Dreier.

Wage work, whether in factories, schools, or settlements, challenged America's social ideology regarding women. As women worked for wages, a tension arose between "virtue" (or the altruistic fulfillment of women's "natural" tendency to nurture and serve) and "independence" (or the desire for self-enhancement).[7] All of my subjects experienced this tension although they lived their lives outside conventional families. Barnum promoted independence for women in tandem with the idea that work and trade union membership would make women better suited to marriage. Dreier and Newman justified better wages and fewer hours for working women with the time-honored goals of improving the "mothers of the race." And Pesotta's conception of the union as a surrogate family distinguished her organizing style. In their own independent lives, these four women found "virtue" in service to humankind.[8]

FEMINISM, SOCIALISM, AND ANARCHISM

Though Barnum, Dreier, Newman, and Pesotta are not simply versions of the same story, all fit comfortably under the umbrella of female labor activism. That is, each found herself aware of the horrific social problems of her age, and each committed herself to programs, policies, and movements she believed would improve the lot of women workers. As such, each could legitimately be called a reformer, but "activist" is equally apt when applied to women who spent the better part of their lives directly and decisively combating social problems.

Like most activists, my four subjects approached methods of reform pragmatically albeit from different political philosophies. But for these women who lived long and active lives, the influence of particular ideas was often stronger at one moment than at another. Pauline Newman, for example, was deeply committed to the socialist critique of capitalism as a young woman but wholeheartedly supported the New Deal during the 1930s. Rose

Pesotta identified herself as an anarchist until the time of her death in 1965, yet she accepted many contemporary ideas about trade unionism as well.

During the activist coming-of-age years for all four, America was teeming with ideas and schemes of social justice and equality. In the lifetimes of these women, the climate changed, but all four remained focused on the practical goals of higher wages, shorter hours, and a healthier work environment. Toward the end of her life, Barnum had almost completed writing a history of the labor movement; Dreier was under surveillance by the FBI for her liberal affiliations; Newman still identified herself as a socialist; and Pesotta remained an anarchist.

Feminism formed an important part of the political landscape inhabited by these four women. Barnum, Newman, and Dreier could easily be called feminists, although the term is an anachronism.[9] They supported female suffrage, joined organizations like the WTUL, and had private lives centered primarily on women. But then as now, feminism was more complicated than a simple checklist could indicate. How, for example, does one characterize Rose Pesotta, who acknowledged the sexism of the labor movement and even railed against it yet never associated with feminist organizations? Pesotta, although she might not be considered feminist according to some definitions in use today, shared a "female consciousness" with Barnum, Dreier, and Newman that expressed her awareness of women's disadvantaged social position.

Of the many types of feminism ascribed to activist women during the Progressive period, one of the oldest and now most contested is social feminism, which infused women's reform and women's rights organizations throughout the nineteenth century and into the twentieth. Social feminists believed that women's essential nature gave them a special social mission.[10] While this belief may underlie the rhetoric common to proponents of temperance and female suffrage,[11] it gives no hint of the political spectrum within feminism, nor does it acknowledge that "women's loyalties and alliances outside of feminism shaped their woman oriented activities."[12] Certainly Pauline Newman's allegiance to socialism and the labor movement was as strong as her commitment to WTUL feminism at points in her life. And she would quite clearly have objected to sharing the label "feminist" with Women's Party members who favored the Equal Rights Amendment (ERA).

Class-conscious working women have always found feminism problematic. Even those thoroughly disenchanted with the male-dominated labor movement still hesitated before joining middle-class women, with their individualistic goals of self-satisfaction and career advancement. Many women workers, among them waitresses and garment workers, in an effort to resolve the tension they felt between a class ethic of mutual obligation and their own need for economic security, expressed a specific working-class feminism.[13] Even as early as 1915, the need to define with greater precision the ideas of women who believed in the essential interconnectedness of the women's movement and the labor movement was apparent. A WTUL activist coined the term "industrial feminism" to express much the same idea that later scholars labeled working-class feminism.[14]

Newman and Pesotta, while influenced by concepts of "working class" and "industrial feminism," found equally strong ideological roots for their activism in the Left and the Jewish labor movement. Despite their disenchantment with the sexism of these organizations, they were inspired by the ideas of equality and social justice that animated socialist and anarchist groups as well as the ILGWU.

ORGANIZATIONS

The women described in the following chapters all expressed and drew upon ideas about work, class, and feminism in an array of organizations. At various points in their lives, the activism of Barnum, Dreier, and Newman, and their specific concern for women's issues, found an outlet in suffrage, the WTUL, socialist groups, and trade unions. Pesotta's political vehicle throughout her life was consistently the labor movement, whose tenets she took great pains to reconcile with her anarchist beliefs. The contrasting choices made by these four women are revealing of them individually and had implications for their private and public lives.

Suffrage, the movement known to Barnum, Dreier, and Newman during their early activist years, underwent a sea change in the late nineteenth century. An infusion of new members, many of them professional women, redirected the movement's goals and strategies. Work became central to suffrage discourse; the demand for the vote was made in terms based on "women's economic contribution and their significance as a group" rather than on the "nineteenth century argument for natural rights and on the individual."[15] Although conservative groups within the movement appealed to some male voters with racist and nativist arguments, the more progressive suffragists, particularly in urban areas, asked for male support on the basis of expediency.[16]

Socialists like Newman, however, realized that female suffrage had the potential to strengthen the political voice not only of working women but of the entire working class. During her early activist years, on street corners, in union halls, and in the pages of the labor press, Newman told men: "For your own sake vote for the suffrage amendment."[17] Pesotta arrived in the United States too late to be involved in suffrage. But if we are to judge by her later political philosophy, she would probably have shared the disdain of her anarchist comrades for this "bourgeois" attempt to enlist women's support for the capitalist state.

Not until the early twentieth century, when a second generation of suffragists came of age, did elite women begin to accommodate working-class women in the movement. The change required the two groups of women to renegotiate their relationship.[18] New attitudes about work and the goals of suffrage attracted some working women to the movement. "Concepts of dignity and equality in the work place" and "the ethic of self-support and lifelong independence" espoused by suffrage leaders like Harriet Stanton Blatch and others appealed to working women, who realized that the vote would give them greater control over labor legislation.[19]

Despite the appeal to workers, class differences formed an almost insuperable barrier in the suffrage movement. At some level, working-class women were being asked whether they felt a primary allegiance to like-minded women or to men, with whom they shared class and often ethnicity.[20] The feminist organization that attempted to resolve the conflict was the Women's Trade Union League, whose members included Barnum, Dreier, and Newman. Founded in 1903, the League attempted to unite elite and working-class women in the effort to organize working women into existing trade unions. Over time, the indifference and often hostility of the labor movement toward women forced League women to adopt labor legislation and the education of workers and consumers as new goals.

The League included in its membership working-class women and their middle-class "allies," so that analysis of cross-class cooperation—or the lack of it—in a women's organization is possible.[21] Most scholars who have directed their attention to the League contend that middle-class "allies" controlled the organization; workers were little sisters to their older and supposedly wiser colleagues. This situation has led Marxist scholars to lament the "cooptation" of working-class leaders like Pauline Newman and her colleague Rose Schneiderman.[22]

Other scholars, concerned more with gender than with class, see the League as the last embodiment of a nineteenth-century female culture, one that after the passage of the suffrage amendment gave way to mixed-sex political activity. These scholars mourn the passing of the culture and its achievements.[23]

The League, though, as it is possible to see through the biographies of Mary Dreier and Pauline Newman in particular, lasted more than thirty years after the passage of the Nineteenth Amendment. During these years, the organization took the lead in providing a language that defined the welfare state as well as the personnel who staffed such agencies as the Department of Labor, the Children's Bureau, and the Women's Bureau. The

League's feminism provided a transition from the goals of the nineteenth-century women's movement to the needs of women, particularly working women, in the twentieth century.[24]

Many League members with working-class backgrounds, like Pauline Newman, came to the League disillusioned by the mere lip service that socialists and trade unionists were giving equality for women. To say that Newman was coopted, though, oversimplifies a complicated process. Politically, in their gravitation toward the League, women like Newman made pragmatic, strategic decisions about how best to help their working sisters. Personally, Newman chose the company of women who provided her with community, emotional support, even respectability. It is interesting that Rose Pesotta, although equally disillusioned, was never more than a nominal member of the League.[25]

The organization that claimed Newman's allegiance and Pesotta's as well was the International Ladies' Garment Workers Union. Founded by Jewish socialists in 1900, it gained its greatest strength following a rash of strikes, the Uprisings, beginning in 1909.[26] Two characteristics set this union apart from most of the others in the American Federation of Labor (AFL): a largely female rank and file and organization on the basis of industry rather than skill (apparel was a mass-production industry).[27]

While the union offered tacit support for women's emancipation, it kept female activists like Pauline Newman and Rose Pesotta confined to secondary roles as organizers and educators. Although Rose Pesotta was finally elected to a top leadership position in the ILGWU, she ultimately resigned in protest against the union's sexism. As supporters of the union and also critics of it, Newman, Pesotta, and other union women offer a valuable perspective on working women from the 1920s onward. Their roles, unlike those of men in the hierarchy, brought them into daily contact with garment workers. As the trade came to include more and more Mexican, Asian, and rural white workers, women like Newman and Pesotta came to represent the interests of the union's constituents best, while remaining the least influential of union bureaucrats.

SEXUALITY

Like other feminist biographers who have reframed the genre of biography, I will highlight questions of personal and private life as well as focusing on public accomplishments. In writing the lives of Alice Henry, Belle Moskowitz, Molly Dewson, Margaret Dreier Robins, Eleanor Roosevelt, and many other woman activists, biographers have argued that public and private life intersect in important ways, and they have thus challenged the approach of traditional biographers, who assume that only the public aspects of their usually male subjects' lives demand our attention. Feminist biographers have shown that insight into the intimate areas of a life can profoundly affect the way in which history remembers a subject.[28]

A hallmark of modern culture, for example, was the newfound awareness of female sexuality. During the nineteenth century, society decreed that "respectable" women were passionless. The advent of Freudian psychology and its popularization in the late nineteenth century, as well as increasing social interaction between women and men, led to a redefinition of women's sexual nature. Women, no longer regarded as passionless, were now assumed to have sexual needs on a par with those of men, but social convention demanded that women's desire be satisfied within marriage. An important consequence of this development was the creation of mutually exclusive categories of heterosexual and homosexual, with heterosexual representing the norm and homosexual a deviation from that norm. In some sense, then, the birth of modern female sexuality also heralded the creation of the lesbian. The intense female relationships of Victorian women, seen by historians as normative, would by modern standards be considered deviant.[29]

But the personal, emotional, and even sexual lives of Barnum, Dreier, Newman, and Pesotta do not readily fit the simple categories of Victorian and modern, heterosexual and homosexual. Like a modern career woman, Gertrude Barnum, about whose personal life little is known, broke off her engagement to an aristocratic lawyer, for she felt he would never understand the work that was so important to her. Mary Dreier and Pauline Newman had women as life companions—Frances Kellor and Frieda Miller, respectively. Yet Dreier was passionately in love with her brother-in-law, and Newman, when young, had various male suitors. Furthermore, Frieda Miller bore the child whom she and Newman raised and in her sixties had an affair with "an Indian gentleman." Rose Pesotta, like other anarchist women, in a series of relationships with men demonstrated her belief in "free unions." In other words, the sexual dimension of my subjects' lives was far more complicated than mere social categories would allow us to believe.

The orientation of their personal lives around women gave Dreier and Newman entrée into a remarkable women's culture of educated, professional, and politically progressive women who shared their values and way of life. The women's network, maintained through letters, around dinner tables, and in summer homes, affected reform legislation during the Progressive and New Deal periods and influenced the formation of the American welfare state. On a personal and emotional level, biographers commenting on Rose Pesotta and Emma Goldman lament their lives outside this female culture with its rich web of support for exceptional women. Yet Pesotta found emotional sustenance through her anarchist friends, with whom she always made contact with during her peripatetic organizing career; her mentor, Emma Goldman, was a constant source of support and encouragement.

All four women were guarded in what they told posterity about themselves and particularly about their personal lives. Consciously or unconsciously, they were engaged in a continual process of self-definition and self-editing. They presented themselves carefully in memoirs, interviews, and essays. Yet each, with the exception of Barnum, left archival materials that could be used to challenge the cautiously constructed images.

A disparity between the public and private selves obliges the biographer to balance the desires of her subject with her responsibility as a scholar. I am reminded of Fannia Cohn sitting before a fire tossing more papers into the flames than went into the boxes destined for the New York Public Library, or Rose Schneiderman's "mania for respectability," which led her to edit her own papers carefully, or the passion with which Pauline Newman late in her life protested the contents of a scholarly article in *Labor History*. I think reformer Molly Dewson would be pleased to see the privileged role given her relationship with Polly Porter in the title of her biography, *Partner and I*.[30]

Like quilts, that quintessentially female art form, feminist biographies are often diligently pieced together from archival scraps.[31] Gertrude Barnum left no papers—we will come to know her through her fiction, her published essays, and the observations of others. Dreier, Newman, and Pesotta were more careful to chronicle their lives for posterity, but like all self-conscious historical subjects, they constructed themselves by choosing what to leave behind.

The four lives in the following pages will, I hope, respond to and illuminate the historiographical questions that I have raised in this introduction. These lives will also generate their own questions about modernity and feminism, however, and about the construction of ladies, immigrants, and workers. A comparative biography will more fully make the point that while women are molded by their generational experiences, the individual acting in history is unique. When we write of lives that share much, the voices in one life sometimes answer the silences in another.[32]

A biographer, with hubris, can evaluate lives and enumerate their failures—Barnum dropped out of reform, Dreier and Newman persisted in support of protective legislation long after it was meaningful, and Pesotta never resolved issues in intimate relationships. Yet more important than such scores on a report card is the fact that these women all were, to adapt a phrase from Linda Gordon, "heroines of their own lives." Each in her own way struggled to attain, for herself and for the women of her time, a goal that was well stated by Mary Dreier's fictional heroine Barbara Richards: "To do," namely to find meaningful work, and "To be," to achieve a sense of self-actualization. As women attempting to do and to be, they defined and tried to solve the central problems of modernity for women. They are our cherished foremothers.

I

Gertrude Barnum

1866–1948

"to become one of us"

In a letter dated 23 June 1945, reformer Gertrude Barnum resumed her acquaintance with Fannia Cohn, executive secretary of the Educational Department of the International Ladies' Garment Workers' Union. Writing from Los Angeles, Barnum recalled their early days in the labor movement and Cohn's "disgust" when Barnum refused to accompany her and organizer Abraham Bisno to "another of those long-drawn-out talk fests of the then New York Socialist Party." Turning to Bisno, Cohn had said in Yiddish, "After all she is not one of us." When Bisno translated the remark, Barnum restrained herself from responding, "I might reply that you, being a late-comer to the U.S., you are not yet really one of us." Although from seemingly different poles of the social spectrum—Cohn and Bisno were immigrant Jews, whereas Barnum was the American-born daughter of a distinguished midwestern family—all three were comrades. Together they organized workers and participated in the vibrant political

milieu of turn-of-the-century America. Yet the tension, indeed the pain, apparent in Barnum's memory of a comment made long ago, tells us much about ethnicity, class, and gender as they were perceived in the early years of the twentieth century. Moreover, it expresses Barnum's sense of authority in defining who was American. Barnum's letter, written near the end of her life, summarizes a political philosophy shared with many activists. Yet her ideas often put her at odds with intensely class-conscious colleagues like Cohn and Bisno. Her letter continued, "My 'religion' is the U.S. brand of democracy. As you know, my interest in the union movement is the same as my interest in the 'woman movement' (Suffrage League, W. Voters, Etc.) and it's Free Speech and Free Press and Equal Opportunity for all regardless of creed, color or ignorance. American democracy emphasizes individual responsibility to see that 'leaders' truly represent their own consciences, hearts and minds. We insist that creative action on the part of all the members of our organizations is the price of liberty, and full 'cooperation' is our ultimate goal."[1]

This chapter explores Gertrude Barnum's lifelong struggle with the contradictions presented by her philosophy. She attempted to reconcile a gendered concept of Americanism, one that combined domesticity and citizenship, with what she perceived as the "otherness" of immigrant working women. Her work in settlements, the labor movement, and the suffrage movement illustrates some of the many conflicts with which reform presented activist women. The vast amount of fiction she published in the labor and reform press between 1905 and 1919 shows that complex desires accompanied social activism for women, particularly during a time when definitions of gender were in flux. Throughout her work, but particularly in her fictional writings, Barnum wrote narratives that reframed femininity so as to incorporate the social reality of wage work for women.

Barnum left no personal papers. We can hear her sometimes acerbic voice through letters to fellow reformers, and we can discern her social philosophy through her published essays and fictions. Despite the silences in her own story, she is an able spokesperson for activists who cared deeply about working women yet still had difficulty transcending their own class-bound definitions of Americanism and woman. Her life aptly introduces a hope-filled time in the American past when social problems seemed solvable and women made claims to full citizenship.

In following Barnum's journey from settlement-house work to the suffrage and labor movements to the unique "cultural work" of her popular fiction, we can further understand the intellectual and political climate of Progressivism, particularly the contributions elite women made to the cause of the working woman. But we can also see the tension between those well-intentioned reformers and the women whose lives they saw scarred by industrialization.

By "women's political culture"—that is, the values and institutions that shaped the involvement of feminists like Barnum in Progressivism—we mean, of course, the values and institutions of middle-class women. Throughout the nineteenth century, women were involved in temperance, moral reform, and women's rights. Women's prominence in evangelical religion legitimized such activity, as did the concept of the "republican mother" who shaped the moral character of future voters (by this concept society politicized women's domestic space). By the turn of the century, reform-minded women had begun to incorporate strategies from men's political culture (the mainstream) into their reform activities. That is, they had begun to rely more on direct action than on moral suasion. In that movement from "margin to mainstream," middle-class women like Barnum, active in feminism and labor reform, attempted to conceptualize and include the ideas and experiences of working-class, often immigrant women in their vision of an ideal America. Barnum, in particular, through her life and writings, offered them a model of American womanhood. Hers was an imperfect effort to synthesize the values and experiences of the middle class and the working class, to unite women and men in meaningful ways. But she and her reform-minded colleagues often found themselves, like Barnum, Cohn, and Bisno, in conflict about who was "one of us."[2]

Barnum found it easy to believe in Americanism. She was born in 1866 into the family of a prominent Illinois judge. We know little of Barnum's early life except that she had an outstanding record at Evanston High School, she attended the University of Wisconsin, and she refused to join young women of her social class in a debutante season. In 1893, she became a "resident" at Chicago's Hull House, America's first settlement house and still its most famous. Given what we know of the first generation of American women to attend college, we can assume that she, like others, sought "work and social identity commensurate with their talents" in the settlement-house movement.[3]

We do not know what specific experience or catalytic event brought Gertrude Barnum to the center of American reform. Did a stunning conversion experience, such as Jane Addams's response to a Spanish bullfight, drive home the need for meaningful work? Or did the growing renown of Hull House as a social experiment and the charismatic presence of the redoubtable Miss Addams herself attract Barnum? Barnum would have had ample opportunity to hear Addams and Ellen Starr, the cofounder of Hull House, who spoke widely before women's groups in Chicago in 1889 to explain their work and to gain support for it. Quite possibly Barnum was part of an audience that heard the "uplift of the masses" rejected with disdain in favor of restoring "communications between classes." Perhaps Barnum found purpose in Addams and Starr's honestly stated mission: "to live in the slums as much to help themselves as to aid the poor."[4]

Most likely Barnum's college years and her apparent dislike for the conventional social life of her class led her to explore the possibilities that settlement-house life offered. Settlements provided direction for educated middle-class women (and for some men) and were also, as Kathryn Kish Sklar has observed, "a perfect structure for women seeking secular means of influencing society because it collectivized their talents, it placed yet protected them among the working immigrants whose lives demanded amelioration and it provided them with access to the male political arena while preserving their independence from male dominated institutions."[5] In other words, the settlement house was not just a base from which reform activity emanated but also a space in which women's political culture flourished and was transformed.

When Barnum came to Hull House in 1893, the settlement was housed in a huge brick building on South Halsted Street. Once an "elegant rural homestead," it had served in the years between 1856 and 1889 as a hospital, a factory, an apartment house, an office building, and a furniture store. But the size and location of the building had led Jane Addams and Ellen Starr to find it suitable as a center in the midst of the Chicago slums. And in its first ten years as a social settlement, Hull House expanded in a jerry-built fashion to include new rooms and new buildings, reflecting the changing function of the settlement itself. By the turn of the century, Hull House came to mean not only the original structure but also an art gallery, coffeehouse, kindergarten, gymnasium, and the Jane Club, a cooperative residence for working women.[6]

Early attempts to educate Hull House neighbors through art history lectures and classical music recitals were quickly supplemented with responses to more immediate neighborhood needs—child care, English instruction, and citizenship classes. The great depression of 1893 exacerbated the already deep poverty of the neighborhood and led to the publication of *Hull House Maps and Papers*, the first American attempt to study nationality and income in a working-class neighborhood. The study marked a dramatic shift to research and political reform activity. By the end of the decade Hull House residents were prominent on the reform scene at both the local and national levels. They found that the most effective brooms for cleaning up the neighborhood were at city hall, in the state legislature, or even in Washington.[7]

Barnum eagerly joined the excitement and innovation that characterized the twenty-five years between the founding of Hull House and the beginning of World War I. Visitors—and there were many during those years—consistently commented on the effervescent atmosphere. Beatrice Webb spoke of "one continuous intellectual and emotional ferment," while Henry Demarest Lloyd suspected that Hull House "might easily make good its claim to be the best club in Chicago."[8] Certainly it was the only club that included women as well as men. Indeed, the female residents always outnumbered males and were quite clearly the most influential members of the settlement.[9]

Dinner was the central social experience of the day for Hull House residents, although it by no means ended the day. As a newcomer, Barnum would have found her idealism tempered by more seasoned residents as workers in the settlement's many operations shared accounts of their day in the free-flowing conversations over dinner. Following dinner, clubs and lectures began as Miss Barnum headed the Lincoln Club, Miss Fryar the Jolly Boy's Club, and Miss Young the advanced Latin class.[10]

Barnum's principal responsibilities while a resident at the settlement were financial and educational. She served as assistant treasurer of the house in 1895 and 1896 and had an office in the "nerve center" of Hull House, the Octagon Room. She also supervised the Older People's Clubs, taught U.S. history in the school extension program, and led the Lincoln Club, a social and literary group for young boys.[11] In the evenings she could be found giving residents and neighbors stereopticon lectures on topics such as "Ireland."[12]

From its beginnings, labor was central to the political concerns of the settlement, and Barnum had ample exposure to trade unions. Trade unions, particularly women's unions, used Hull House rooms for meetings and get-togethers. The settlement's interest in labor was obvious not only from the Labor Museum, which preserved immigrant crafts, but also from frequent meetings of trade unions in the settlement's meeting rooms.[13] The Dorcas Federal Labor Union, for example, enticed women workers to join unions in their trades with the reward of pleasant social events.[14] By the time of Barnum's arrival in 1893, the settlement had already assisted a strike of shirtmakers and an organizing drive among cloakmakers. During the next decade, Jane Addams and Florence Kelley, in particular, set the direction for labor reform by extensive lobbying for labor legislation at both the state and federal levels. Barnum soon saw that the political solutions to many egregious social problems were to be found in the labor movement and readily became a spokesperson for its point of view. The philosophy of English trade unionism influenced her sense of the usefulness of unions more than the ideas of Karl Marx. As a contemporary explained, "It was the approach of a few people getting together, binding themselves together, not selling each other down the river . . . telling the bosses they wouldn't work unless they paid them a decent wage, gave them reasonable hours and did not make them pay for the thread that they used."[15]

While her noted colleagues pursued a legislative strategy, Barnum during her settlement years worked as a propagandist and an unaffiliated organizer. Frances Perkins, later to be secretary of labor, remembered Barnum as a "rich, fearless and highly educated woman" who spoke forcefully and emotionally to sweatshop "bundle workers." We have no record of the workers' response to the "tall and magnificent" Barnum, but her remarks stunned Perkins. She recalled: "I remember it because, as I was quite a young girl, I had never heard a labor union speech. . . . At that time I thought trade unions were an evil to be avoided. . . . You did good to the poor with charitable relief, friendly visiting, pleasant Sunday afternoons in Hull House, mother's clubs. . . . I was just on the verge of becoming acquainted with the world as it truly is."[16]

In 1897, Barnum left the settlement "on the verge of nervous prostration."[17] The cause of her condition is unclear. It may have been the result of the frenetic pace of settlement-house life. It may have been in the wake of her broken engagement to an "aristocratic lawyer." A sister resident wrote that Barnum "induced" her fiancé "rather against his will" to live in the Halsted Street neighborhood. They had planned (or perhaps, more accurately, she had planned) to take a modest apartment after their marriage as she continued her work at the settlement. But she soon came to realize that her beau's lukewarm support for the venture made it a "doubtful experiment." Madeline Sikes wrote that Barnum "decided after all that she didn't care for him as much as she does for the work down here and she could see that he would never be in sympathy with it."[18] It is more surprising that Barnum expected her future husband to accommodate himself to her work than that their wedding plans failed. Pioneering professional women of her generation by and large found that marriage brought their professional activities to an end.

Whatever the cause of her "collapse," Barnum dropped from public view for almost five years. Possibly she traveled; possibly she returned to her family's home in Evanston. In any case she eventually returned to the work that had been so important to her at Hull House. In 1902 she became head resident at the Henry Booth House in Chicago, a settlement founded by the Ethical Humanist Society in Chicago's congested North Ward.

When she left Hull House, she left a surrogate family as well as a crucible in which the political awareness of reformers took shape. There Barnum interacted on a daily basis not only with dynamic social reformers but also with women who worked in Chicago's garment shops and meat-processing plants. By the time Barnum became head resident of Henry Booth House, she had honed her political sensibilities under Jane Addams's tutelage, ideas well described by historian Kathryn Kish Sklar as "in but not of the Social Gospel stream, advancing political solutions to social problems that were fundamentally ethical or moral."[19]

Barnum's new home was located in the ninth ward, an area densely populated by newly arrived Jews, Italians, Bohemians, Lithuanians, and Poles. Henry Booth House was small by Hull House standards—seven residents as compared with fifty-one at Hull House. But Booth House, founded almost ten years after Hull House opened its doors, showed the influence of the older settlement in its explicitly stated mission: "to secure better streets, improved public sanitary conditions, better housing and the extension of school work." Like Hull House, it also maintained an array of clubs and classes for women and children, "conducted several campaigns against evil moral conditions; and tried to develop a more tolerant feeling between the neighborhood races."[20]

Barnum's tenure at Henry Booth House was brief, but when it ended, her reasons for leaving settlement-house work were clear. She agreed with Walter Lippmann and others that "Hull House (and settlements like it) cannot remake Chicago." In 1905 she wrote: "I myself have graduated from the Settlement into the trade union. As I became more familiar with the conditions around me, I began to feel that while the Settlement was undoubtedly doing a great deal to make the lives of working people less grim and hard, the work was not fundamental. It introduced into their lives books and flowers and music, and it gave them a place to meet and see their friends or leave their babies when they went out to work, but it did not raise their wages or shorten their hours."[21]

Barnum's quest for bread rather than roses for workers set her on a new course, but ten years in settlement work had left their mark. During that practical apprenticeship in social reform, she observed the daily life of the working poor, absorbed Jane Addams's philosophy of social democracy, and became skilled in techniques of public speaking and community organization. At the same time she came to know the limitations of the settlement as an agent of social change. Wage work for women and its attendant unregulated qualities drew her attention to the labor movement.

Barnum's strong belief in a democratic labor movement extended to the idea of mixed-sex unions.[22] Barnum soon realized, however, that animosity or indifference was more common between women and men in the labor movement than cooperation.[23] The apparent need for a separate women's labor organization led Barnum in 1903 to become a founder and organizer for the Women's Trade Union League. The WTUL, an organization initially sponsored by the American Federation of Labor, aimed to unite working-class women and middle-class "allies" in organizing women workers.[24] When the League became disenchanted with direct organizing and turned its attention to suffrage, Barnum was employed as a special agent for the International Ladies' Garment Workers' Union, where she spent her time organizing, publicizing, and writing.

In 1905, WTUL organizers targeted the garment trades because of their large and unorganized female workforce. Barnum's first assignment was to join Rheta Childe Dorr, a journalist and a reformer, in organizing striking laundry workers in Troy.[25] Barnum followed Dorr's activities in the laundry strike by organizing corset workers in Illinois, textile workers in Fall River, Massachusetts, garment workers in Chicago, button workers in Iowa, and cloak and skirt makers in the Great Uprising in Cleveland. All in all, she participated in eight strikes during her time as an organizer.

Despite differences in the trades, the issues targeted were often the same: low wages or low rates for piecework, filthy work spaces, speedups, and, frequently, sexual harassment. In Muscatine, Iowa, for example, the disclosure of sexual harassment and venereal disease so shocked public sensibilities that, the union claimed, it resulted in jail sentences for twelve striking workers. Arriving on the scene, Barnum struck a note of moral outrage: "The Union alone can keep up the good work of protecting the helpless young country girls who are lured from their farm homes by inviting advertisements and are then left at the mercy of the greed of men—greed for money and greed for the flower of our young womanhood."[26] Barnum's rhetorical choices—the innocent country girl, the unprincipled man, the seduction trope— were staples of reform literature. Women, at least at this point in Barnum's thinking, needed protection, which could be provided only by the union (whose male members were apparently uncorrupted by "greed").

Whatever the issues and however similar the discourse, in each of these strikes of unorganized female workers, Barnum tried to win public opinion in support of the organization of workers. Her two-pronged strategy was first to enlist the moral authority of clergy, university professors, journalists, and others on the side of the strikers and then to mobilize consumers to boycott products from unorganized factories. As with so much of Barnum's activity, this approach was marked by the distinctive hallmarks of progressive reform: belief in the power of education and of public opinion; the underlying assumption that the professions were neutral observers of the class struggle; and faith in the unrealized potential of consumers to effect social change.[27]

Barnum's approach did not always sit well with more class-conscious organizers or with women of her own background. In 1911 she expressed amazement "to learn that society women, club women and church societies sat passively through the Cleveland strike while the employers refused to arbitrate and insisted upon settling issues by the force of starvation and false arrests and intimidation by hired thugs and sluggers."[28] Struck by Barnum's naivete, Pauline Newman, a working-class union organizer, sneered, "G.B. is no more able to do this job than I am to be a dancing master."[29]

Barnum developed and deployed her attitudes toward reform in settlements and strikes—two of the political spaces in which she encountered working women. The third political space that brought women of different classes together during the Progressive period was the suffrage movement. Although there was strong anti-immigrant sentiment in some corners of the movement, Barnum was in the vanguard of suffrage activists, who believed that the movement would be revitalized through the recruitment of working (read immigrant) women.

The idea that the ranks should be opened reflected dramatic changes in the leadership, strategies, and goals of the women's rights movement. In the years following 1894, younger professional women had taken up the torch passed by Stanton and Anthony and had focused flagging energies on the demand for female suffrage through a federal amendment. As previously noted, the reformulated movement attempted to renegotiate the relationship between elite and working-class women. Historically, women's rights activists had viewed women of the lower classes as social charges. Now, however, the common experience of work joined professional and working-class women at least on a symbolic level. Speaking for the new generation, Harriet Stanton Blatch and others tried to include the industrial workers, especially trade union women, in the suffrage struggle. The incorporation of the working-class woman carried with it, however, an implicit threat to class relations. Many middle-class Americans feared the enfranchisement of the lower classes and their potential voting power.

At the 1906 convention of the National Woman Suffrage Association (NWSA), the class-inclusive faction of the movement clearly carried the day. Clara Barton and Julia Ward Howe, nineteenth-century icons of the women's movement, were honored participants, and one highlight of the convention was the appearance of Susan Anthony, fragile yet luminescent. Still, these pioneers were like nineteenth-century tableaux in contrast to the contemporary voices that resounded through the convention. Anna Howard Shaw criticized antisuffrage male "Oracles" such as Cardinal Gibbons, former president Cleveland, and President Roosevelt.[30] Florence Kelley spoke movingly of child labor, and the College Women's Equal Suffrage League was featured in the proceedings. The general celebration of the modern woman primed the audience for Barnum's address, entitled "Women as Wage Earners." As she took the podium, Barnum asked her audience where the wage-earning women were. They were certainly not at the convention, and they were certainly not participating in the suffrage fight. Yet the experience of women in trade unions would be a great asset to the movement, and the ballot itself would empower the working woman to change working conditions, which, Barnum claimed, were literally destroying her, body and soul.

By the time Barnum pronounced her valediction that "our hope as suffragists lies with these strong willed working women," she had articulated the obvious differences between women of the working class and women of leisure: "We have been preaching to them, teaching them, 'rescuing' them, doing almost everything for them except knowing them and working with them for the good of the common country." Finally, Barnum spoke of the greater need of wage-earning women for the franchise. Women of her own class, she said, simply "suffer from the insult of its refusal."[31]

Barnum's point of view—that the perspective of working-class women was critical to the women's movement—made her part of a sea change in the national suffrage movement. She challenged the conception of womanhood that had grounded the movement throughout the nineteenth century. By the time Barnum addressed the "leisure class" of the 1906 NWSA convention, however, she believed that class had created a growing fissure between elite, often educated women who controlled the movement and wage-earning women whom Barnum and others eagerly sought to include in the suffrage ranks.

Yet while Barnum valorized the "strong will" of working women, she never spoke of what might divide them from other women. The goals, life experiences, and social context that women did not share passed without comment. It was as though she expected the icon of "work" to transcend competing political and cultural values.

It could be said of Barnum, as it has been said of other suffragists, that she rewrote feminism in its modern form, around work. Barnum's position was not rooted solely in ideology but followed logically from her experience.[32] By 1906, she had spent more than a decade in settlement-house work, interacting on a daily basis with immigrants and wage-earning women. During 1905 she represented the WTUL in at least three strikes of women workers, working alongside union organizers and other seasoned reformers. But Barnum saw working women as more than strategic allies in the suffrage fight. One historian has written that, with the valorizing tone of her convention address, Barnum had come to regard "wage-earning women less as victims to be succored, than as exemplars to their sex."[33]

The shift in perspective can be linked at least in part to the way in which militant suffragists were calling for changes in the bourgeois definition of womanhood.[34] No longer was the ideal the "true woman," determined to extend her moral authority to all society through reform and the ballot. The "new woman" worked, was educated, and claimed the ballot on the basis of her equality with men rather than her difference from them. Although factory workers and shop girls were hardly part of the new woman ideal, the fact that they worked for wages made them a progressive social force in the eyes of many reformers.[35]

It was a significant problem for suffrage activists to include working-class women in the movement, but it could not afford to alienate its wealthy supporters. By 1910 the suffrage movement was still in the hands of women of wealth, many of whom understood that an enfranchised working class posed a potential political threat. The tension between those who wished to bring working women into the movement and those who wanted to exclude them was never really resolved. As historian Ellen DuBois has written, "From the beginning . . . class was the contradiction at the suffrage movement's heart."[36]

If Barnum felt the contradiction, she did not say so. Despite her own privileged background, Barnum continued to work vigorously to bring the less privileged into the suffrage ranks. In 1917, two years before the passage of the suffrage amendment, she became chairwoman of the Labor Suffrage Committee of the Massachusetts Women's Suffrage Association. By that time reformers had mobilized significant labor support for the suffrage cause, particularly in Massachusetts and New York, and had succeeded in gaining legislative approval for votes for women in 1914 and 1915. Since about 1914, moreover, the Women's Trade Union League had shifted its reform strategy from organizing workers to suffrage and protective legislation. The task between 1915 and 1919 was to keep the support of labor alive and to convey to the voting public a sense that victory was inevitable in the fight for a federal amendment.

Barnum entered the Massachusetts suffrage campaign reluctantly. While she was certain that victory was assured, she also felt that organizing among a working-class constituency should be done by the families of trade union men. Her fear that the "enemies of labor are rapidly organizing women and immigrants at this very moment in a way that threatens labor-legislative interests" brought her into the campaign. Writing to AFL president Samuel Gompers, Barnum outlined her goals and strategy: first she intended to unionize the suffrage office, and then she planned to make a men's and women's suffrage committee—"putting it up to the labor men to make good in practice their theory that women should have the vote." Her stated goal was "to double labor's vote." But most important, she aimed to Americanize the immigrant woman and to train her for citizenship, "laying stress on 'loyalty' to the government, etc."[37] Barnum seemed unaware that doubling labor's vote at a time when labor included significant elements critical of the United States might not be the best way to ensure loyalty to the government!

When speaking to middle-class audiences, Barnum soft-pedaled the message of doubling labor's vote. Ladies taking tea at an afternoon reception in Boston heard Barnum play her theme in a different key: what was needed was to Americanize Americans by passing suffrage that would guarantee full citizenship for women. She sketched a plan to "get in touch with some of the finest types of inspiring and capable foreign born women and cooperate with them in training newcomers for citizenship." The work experience of the foreign-born made them a "great asset" in fighting the "horrors" of industry.[38] These working-class women, in other words, would infuse the suffrage movement with an energy and a perspective drawn from the experience of wage labor, but in Barnum's vision, they would not challenge the basic tenets of American democracy. This approach quite neatly forestalled the objections of the suffragists—and presumably the ladies at the Boston tea—who would exclude the working class from the vote. Whether or not Barnum's view represented political reality is another question.

Female activists with working-class roots and socialist sensibilities hardly agreed with Barnum. Women like Pauline Newman, a Socialist Party and trade union activist, included female suffrage in a constellation of political demands aimed at empowering the working class. While she shared Barnum's concern "to double labor's vote," for Newman doing so involved consolidating working-class strength, not making workers "one of us." Newman and others explicitly objected to suffragist agendas that would make woman "a near divinity." Newman felt strongly that suffrage and "all else" would be won "much more quickly and effectively when we fight out the issues with honesty and fair play to all and give men a square deal."[39]

Newman's last-quoted comment illustrates the sharp divide between activists on the suffrage question. The women's movement, which had promised to mobilize enfranchised women into a reform-oriented voting bloc, could never transcend the fault line that separated middle-class and working-class women. Feminists failed to resolve the contradictions posed by the distinct political cultures of the socialist class analysis represented by Newman and the liberal reform tradition presented by Barnum. The fight for votes for women occurred at a historical moment when class distinctions were particularly apparent, but it also offered the opportunity to transcend those differences in a joint effort for women's rights. Even women like Barnum who genuinely wanted to include workers in the suffrage movement wanted to do so on their own terms—wanted workers "to become one of us."

Barnum and Newman clearly presented the suffrage message to working-class voters in different ways, as we have seen. There were, in addition, other ways in which class figured in urban suffrage campaigns. The very masses feared by some suffragists made the difference between victory and defeat in such states as New York, Massachusetts, and California.[40] Like Newman, many working-class men understood that women, once enfranchised, could wield considerable political power. Not all, of course, supported the suffrage cause. Many could not see beyond traditional notions of women's social role. In immigrant communities in New York City, for example, immigrant men tended to vote for female suffrage if women in their communities were employed in unionized work and if daily life brought them consistently into contact with working women.[41]

Suffrage was, of course, not the only area in which Barnum demonstrated a blindness to the complexities of class. She was one of first Americans to accept and write about the concept of industrial democracy. By the time that Barnum published her 1912 essay "How Industrial Peace Has Been Brought About in the Clothing Trades," she had evolved a coherent social philosophy imbued with the social thought of her day. Like her mentor, Jane Addams, and many other progressives, Barnum studied the industrial warfare around her and pronounced it unnecessary. There was, to her mind, no reason why management and labor could not recognize the mutual benefits of industrial peace and lie down together like the lion and the lamb.

The terms Barnum used to describe this process, "industrial democracy" and the "industrial ballot," grew directly from a powerful faith in social democracy that was like a religion for the Progressives. Social democracy as articulated in both Europe and the United States during the early twentieth century was characterized by knowledge based on experience, a commitment to extend the democratic principle of equality from the civil and political spheres to the entire society and economy, reform that was gradual and constitutional, and a focus on proximate reforms rather than on ultimate ends.[42]

But social democracy had a slippery chameleonic quality. At its most expansive, social democracy underscored notions of Fabian socialism held by many Progressives; yet for others, like Walter Lippmann, genuine democracy was an absurd ideal. For Barnum, the social democratic ethos was best realized in plans for industrial democracy.

Industrial democracy had a long intellectual history but became a key topic of debate only during the Progressive Era.[43] Barnum's ideas on the subject may have been influenced by Sidney and Beatrice Webb's publication of *Industrial Democracy* in 1897. Industrial reformers in the United States were attracted to the Webbs' vision of an ideal society: "Industry would be governed on a functional basis: consumers to determine what goods industry should produce, managers to determine how goods were to be produced, and unions to determine the conditions of production, with the State playing a partnership role in every enterprise in order to protect the interests of the community as a whole."[44] By 1918–1919, industrial democracy figured prominently in the discourse of industrial relations in the United States.

Barnum's reading of industrial democracy reinforced her conviction that workers' and managers' interests did not conflict. Although Barnum saw the hope of the women's movement lay "with these strong willed working women" whom she had encountered in settlements, strikes, and the suffrage movement, she remained unpersuaded that class struggle was inevitable.

Interviewing industrialist Morris Black for a union paper, Barnum gave more clues to her own thought than to his. Her essay shows how she worked through some of the contradictions. Barnum told Black that her association with Hull House had led her to the "conclusion that the trouble with the neighborhood was mainly industrial injustice." To counter this injustice, she planned "to create public opinion for arbitration and the Industrial Ballot" by enlisting the support of clergy, university faculties, and women's clubs.[45] For Barnum, the industrial ballot was a metaphor for the joint interests of workers, owners, and consumers in industry.[46]

The same faith in the cooperative spirit was illustrated fictionally by Barnum's parable "The Living Skeleton and the Stout Reformer." The Living Skeleton consumptively coughed her way through her days in a textile mill. The Stout Reformer (who was also, for narrative convenience, the mill president) was not insensitive to the presence of the "white plague" in the mills but felt that an expansion of the county fresh air farm would provide for its victims. The Living Skeleton drew the Stout Reformer into the mill to demonstrate to him that workplace conditions were the source of the disease. With a new awareness, the portly entrepreneur took the "skinney hand" of the emaciated worker in his "fat one" and shouted: "By George, I won't stand for all this. . . .

you were dead right. We're manufacturing death faster than cloth. I guess this is about the best place to begin the fresh air cure for tuberculosis." In the story, the worker takes the lead in instructing the owner, but once he has been enlightened, class differences recede as employer and worker together strive for a cleaner and healthier society.[47]

Barnum's clearest statement on industrial democracy appears in a series of essays on the Protocol of Peace.[48] The protocol was a collective bargaining agreement between the International Ladies' Garment Workers' Union and New York manufacturers that settled a protracted cloakmakers' strike in New York City. Hailed as a landmark in industrial relations, the protocol was a high-water mark for the principles of industrial democracy.[49] Barnum welcomed and popularized the protocol in several articles. For her, it represented cherished ideals of Americanism applied to grim industrial problems—a balance of power between employer, employees, and public interest; arbitration rather than the "waste, suffering and bitterness of strikes." She wrote approvingly of the ILGWU's efforts to mobilize consumers through "circular letters and public addresses, church audiences, women's clubs, suffrage and teacher's associations, benefit societies, trade unions and socialist organizations . . . to insist that merchants shall supply their patrons with 'Protocol' garments." Barnum expected widespread adoption of protocol agreements to end the sexual harassment that she found so disturbing in her factory investigations. Ideally, in protocol shops a board of grievances would resolve a worker's complaint without the worker's possible loss of a job.[50]

Unfortunately, we do not know whether the private Barnum was as equally and as uncritically enthusiastic about the protocol as Barnum the writer. It is difficult to imagine that a woman who had been as close to industrial workers as Barnum could so naively accept the large yet simple limitations of the protocol. Historian Melvyn Dubofsky reminds us: "Ideals of equality and impartial public intervention proved meaningless when industrial disputants were of unequal strength."[51]

Barnum believed that the industrial ballot would level the playing field between unequal players in industrial relations. Her belief in this concept was so strong that she viewed scientific management as compatible with industrial democracy. Her contributions to *100%: The Efficiency Magazine* put her at odds with many trade unionists, who viewed scientific management as yet another attempt to wrest control of work from the workers. Barnum wrote that Taylorism could be incorporated into a scheme of industrial democracy. Citing the Shipley Report on "Efficiency by Consent" and J. A. Hobson's writings on guild socialism, Barnum suggested that workers be given an "industrial ballot" to infuse the "consent of the governed" into the scientifically managed factory.[52]

Barnum's growing reputation as an authority on industrial matters as well as, we might say, her growing compatibility with mainstream political thought won her a seat on the federal Industrial Relations Commission in 1914 and a position as assistant director of the Investigation Service for the Department of Labor in 1918–1919. In 1919, Barnum settled in California, where she continued to be involved in reform organizations such as the League of Women Voters until her death in 1948.[53]

Barnum's life, beliefs, and strategies for reform embody seemingly irresolvable contradictions of class and gender—as well as showing how women's and men's political culture came together during the early years of the twentieth century. Barnum clearly belonged to the generation of women who found community in the settlement experience and brought the values of social housekeeping to social reform. In other words, the women's political culture born at Hull House found expression in her commitment to suffrage and her organizing of industrial workers. But her writing included notions of individualism and industrial democracy that were drawn from mainstream male political culture, notions that rested on a sense that women were the same as men rather than different from them.

Similarly, Americanization for Barnum meant the inclusion of immigrants into the American political fold, support of their strikes, and the availability of wage work for women. But Barnum's concept of Americanization rested on contradictions as well. Her desire to include immigrants in the polity was tempered by her drive to "make them one of us"; her support for strikers coexisted with her belief in an industrial democracy that would prevent strikes; and her defense of the right to work for women coexisted with her promotion of marriage as an appropriate social goal for women.

Many Progressives shared Barnum's views toward social investigation, education, and legislative reform, but comparatively few lived and worked among lower-class women and knew as well as Barnum how they experienced work and home. Despite this proximity, though, she exemplified the failure of the reformers to create a genuine coalition of middle-class and working-class women that might have challenged dominant social ideas about women.

The failure occurred on several levels. By the 1920s women had "lost the basis for a separate political culture."[54] The most obvious reason was the breakup of the suffrage coalition into organizations with different political agendas. Feminists who had been players on the labor reform scene through the Progressive years formed separate camps on the issue of protective legislation. Women associated with the National Women's Party sponsored an Equal Rights Amendment; feminists of the WTUL continued to support and defend protective legislation as the most efficient means of improving "life and labor" for working women. Although Barnum never joined the Women's Party, she was a vigorous critic of the legislative strategy of the WTUL.

Underlying these political positions was a complicated and gendered cultural subtext that can best be explored through Barnum's writings, especially her fiction. Barnum was not an architect of a political point of view, but through her prescriptive writings she promoted a variety of views and definitions of womanhood. As we have seen, she valorized the independence of the working woman particularly in her efforts to win suffrage, yet she often expressed moral outrage as she described "helpless young country girls" in need of protection. She also divided the category "woman" into wage earners empowered by work and trade union experience and their more leisured sisters. Finally, while she portrayed women as victims of a voracious industrial machine, her feminism required her to tell readers that the operators of the machine were "greedy men."

Barnum, as *Life and Labor* reported, "did yeoman service in interpreting the troubles of the girls to their more comfortably placed sisters." Her role as mediator and translator placed her in various different positions in the world of labor and reform in the early twentieth century. During the thirteen years she spent as an organizer and publicist for the WTUL and the ILGWU, Barnum was involved in at least eight major strikes of female workers. While her explicit goal in each instance was to organize women workers into unions, that goal was always accompanied by her efforts to involve elite women in the struggle. Women's clubs heard her appeal to consumers to buy garments "made under fair conditions"; readers of reform publications were introduced to individual workers whose lives had been scarred by squalid industrial conditions; and middle-class audiences often met workers coached by Barnum to deliver their pro-union message.

But the medium that Barnum chose for her most original—yet seemingly most contradictory—portrait of the working "girl" was the fiction she wrote for the labor and reform press. In scores of short stories, tales, and fables she sketched a model of womanhood that stood in distinct contrast to the nineteenth-century ideal of the "true woman"—pious, pure, submissive, and sentimental. Her fiction can be read as a primer of reform ideology regarding women workers.[55] The fiction, though, is far from social realism: it mirrors the values of feminist reformers more clearly than it depicts the world of the woman worker.

A "Third Sex"—that is, a woman worker who herself demands protection—never appears in Barnum's stories. The Barnum girl is spunky, down-to-earth, and brimming over with common sense and good cheer. The moral calculus of Barnum's fictional world rewarded such behavior with admiration, romance, and financial success. In one story, Patsy, who was willing to design valentines to support her more serious art, triumphs over her uncompromising friend Millicent. The handsome junior partner in the valentine firm, a "big shouldered stunner," emerges as a fellow painter, potential suitor, and buyer of Patsy's serious painting.[56] In another story, Barnum made a rather extravagant claim for cheerful behavior: "If girls have spirit enough, they can change working conditions by looking pleasant. A group of smiling girls can get things from employers which would never be willingly granted to glum girls."[57]

The lengthy story "Her Sister's Leavings" featured alternative models of manhood as well as appropriate values for women. Sisters Marion and Laura were engaged to Cornelius Stanton and Ted Norgrove, respectively. The domineering Stanton had a limousine, polo ponies, and a fondness for champagne suppers. Norgrove was a journalist with a taste for life's simple pleasures— swimming, fishing, and exploring the coast. In the course of a plot that includes a harrowing chase with a runaway horse, the sisters finally exchange fiancés. And although observers certainly felt that Marion would make the "better match" with the aristocratic Stanton, and Laura took "her sister's leavings" with Norgrove, the reader is left with no doubts as to who will have the happier, more fulfilling life.[58] Like much popular fiction, Barnum's story of Marion, Laura, and their suitors appealed to her reader's escapist fantasies. The romantic narrative was well known to readers, usually female, of popular fiction, who anticipated the marital conclusion. But as Janice Radway and others point out, the romance, which on the face of it limits women's vision, can also empower.

Rereading "Her Sister's Leavings," for example, we can see that Laura assertively moves from one beau to another. Rather than selecting her mate on the basis of future wealth and security, she expresses a more modern preference for companionate marriage with its goal of happiness and emotional well-being. Finally, the female characters do not work for wages but live in a more carefree environment that their laboring audience might aspire to.

Not all of Barnum's stories use the escapist device of a setting far from the reality of tenement and factory. Many are situated in factories and shops. Work is a simple place in the Barnum canon, though, uncomplicated by the squalor and sexual harassment described in her essays. Yet even in these idealized settings, workers still need higher wages and shorter hours. Obstacles to improvement are often unenlightened girls whose concern with novels, political theory, or social life has kept them from hearing the union message. A "deep-eyed Russian girl" with literary aspirations is advised, "The best kind of literature and journalism for working people to take up is signed Trade Agreements." Once the workers have been organized, their claims are readily met by employers, and they find themselves in a class of self-respecting "girls with will-power behind their pink cheeks, who can open their mouths and put a price on themselves, and a good price, too."[59]

As in nineteenth-century social ideology, though, women figure differently than men. Their emotionalism and superior moral sensibilities set them apart from men but complement men's more rational natures. In an untitled story, for example, a woman responds to the measured tones of a man's speech with "the passionate gleam of dark blue eyes, the passionate appeal and support of a woman's transparent soul."[60] And in "Fortune Tellers," one girl lectures another on the foolishness of consulting fortune tellers rather than giving a few cents to unions to get "protection in the shape of sick benefits, higher wages and labor laws." Her advice falls on deaf ears, however, for the listener has "an exceptional feminine brain. The credulity of girls is not half suspected by the laity, though it is freely exploited by an unscrupulous fraternity of fakers."[61]

Barnum's stories elaborated on industrial democracy and Americanization but refracted these ideas through the prism of romance. The story of a fictive strike in a Massachusetts mill town features Beatrice, a well-born woman who had taken on worker's roles as a housemaid and mill worker to investigate industrial conditions. She concludes—without surprise to faithful Barnum readers—that the mobilization of public opinion should lead to an arbitration board that will settle Shuttleville's problems. Beatrice's life is complicated by a budding romance with Mr. Welbourne, the mill owner. She resists his advances until finally his passion overcomes her reservations. In the story's romantic conclusion, Mr. Welbourne exhorts his future bride: "Let us work together to free the [wage] slaves, and let us leave strong children to work after we are gone." Beatrice pledges that she will help him "to become an American."[62]

The story of the Shuttleville lovers, although seemingly conforming to a familiar romantic strategy, actually subverts the romantic formula in several important ways. The female protagonist, not the male, is the "scientific" investigator. She will define "American," maintain control of her emotions during their courtship, and convert her suitor to a politically liberal point of view. In other words, the woman has taken on many characteristically "male" attributes—rationality, restraint, and the ability to make cultural definitions.

Barnum's subversive heroine, of course, hardly mirrors the working girls for whom her author created her. She is a sort of class cross-dresser, like the various middle-class reformers who went "undercover" during the Progressive period to investigate workplace conditions. Although they appeared to be workers, they carried their class privilege into the workplace with them. Yet before we too quickly reject the notion of Barnum's fiction as socially regressive, let us consider the ideas of Michael Denning, who has written about mass-produced dime novels and working-class culture. Denning asks us to see ideology "as a set of stories one tells oneself to situate oneself in the world, to name the characters and map the terrain of the social world."[63] Barnum, whether consciously or unconsciously, successfully resolved many of the contradictory elements in her own political life. And by revisioning romance and the male/female dyad in the romantic formula, Barnum did not wrest the pleasure of the familiar ro-

mantic fantasy from her readers but rather allowed them the satisfaction of romantic closure and wish fulfillment while introduc-
ing new gender role concepts.

Given the "spunky" character of most of Barnum's heroines,
one would assume that they could be described as autonomous
as well. But Barnum expressed ambivalent views about autonomy. In her column "Gertrude Barnum Talks to Girls," written
for the *New York World*, autonomy received her uncritical endorsement. She criticized the working "girl" who depended on
"settlements, philanthropists and reformers instead of paddling
her own canoe and being under obligations to no one." In a striking departure from the romantic conclusions of much of her fiction, Barnum went on to describe this composite girl "as she
scans the landscape in search of some man to marry and 'take care
of her' with no sense of shame at not being able to take care of
herself."[64] Barnum's criticism of the dependent "girl" foreshad-
owed her rejection of protective legislation—the woman worker
should not characterize herself as a third sex, a being who has
"lost faith in a chance to improve the conditions of the members
by working with men."[65] Barnum promoted a belief that work
and femininity were not incompatible. It was a belief that implicitly denied any tension between women and men either at work
or in the labor movement. "The Pig-headed Girl"—the tale with
which I began this book—was in many ways the model Barnum
heroine. She differed from the reluctant canoe paddler in one important respect—when it came time to marry, she did marry, but
she wed a man of her choice. Like her creator, who imagined a
modern marriage with her "aristocratic lawyer" fiancé in Chicago's slums, the pigheaded girl never risked intimacy and companionship while she found fulfillment in work.

Varied in plots, unrelentingly romantic in tone, these stories
propose a clear model of womanhood—independent, outspoken,
generous, practical, and often self-supporting. It is a model at
odds with Barnum's own life. She enjoyed an independence made
possible by a private income and lived largely in the company
of women rather than men. Her vision may have embodied the

aspirations of her readers, but did it represent the reality of their lives?

One could argue that Barnum's stories offer an alternative vision of how things could be and, given what we know of economic opportunity for women during the early twentieth century, clearly were not. The pigheaded girl, for example, operated in a sort of free labor market—free, that is, from the constraints of marginal jobs for women. Nevertheless, her activities, and those of other characters, still take place in a traditional context: their goal is always marriage.

The stories legitimate work for women and feminize union activity but also accept marriage, male bosses, and the reality of the power that men exercise over women. In terms of appearance, courtship mores, and the verbal interchange between women and men, Barnum's stories promoted a conventional ideal of respectability. Her fiction also firmly and attractively incorporated wage work into the female life cycle along with marriage. But the primary goal for women—marriage—and the life pattern of alternating wage work and domestic work constituted the domestic and reproductive circumstances of most working women as well as of the pigheaded girl and her fictional sisters.

Still, perhaps we should not concern ourselves with the fit between Barnum's imaginary world and reality. Michael Denning reminds us that each fictional formula "has its moment of success, when it is able to offer convincing symbolic resolutions to social contradictions, and its historical limits, when the pressure of the real reveals its plots and resolutions to be merely imaginary."[66]

Barnum's fictions, then, tried to resolve the layers of contradiction found in her other writings. On the one hand, labor should speak with its own voice, as she so strongly stated during the Massachusetts suffrage campaign. On the other hand, working women were implicitly encouraged to model their behavior on the pigheaded girl, a romantic construction of what Barnum saw as the self-actualizing potential of wage work for women. If one set Barnum's "exposé" essays and her fiction side by side, one would conclude that they had been written by different authors.

In the former pieces, women are victims, while in the latter, they emerge as winners.

Who was the "Perfect lady" (as Barnum entitled one newspaper article)? Certainly not the "rich, leisure class women [who] adore parrots, puppies and other stupid pets." But neither was she the stenographer who "snubs the shop girl; the shop girl [who] snubs the factory girl, and all women [who] feel superior to domestic servants."[67] She exhorted her readers to strive for "broad human companionship," for the "girls of today must build up a true society of the splendid America of tomorrow. We must pin our faith to the power of their quick sympathy, their tact, their idealism to break down the foolish barriers of caste, and teach the children true American principles." The "perfect lady," then, had a unique social mission—to instill democratic principles in future generations, thus shaping an egalitarian America. Her maternal role was clearly linked to larger political purposes and to the welfare of the state. The ideal woman embodied the religion of democracy that Barnum articulated to Fannia Cohn some thirty years later.[68]

Barnum's fiction feminized the meaning of work. By choosing a romantic genre, she made work as well as political action and independent behavior palpable and palatable to working-class readers. Immigrant men envisioned the New World as a place where they could achieve material success. For immigrant women, however, America was where marriage could be a romantic choice rather than merely arranged. Barnum, whether consciously or unconsciously, addressed these hopes.[69]

In the process Barnum infused the hopeful and corporatist vision of the Progressives with gender. She became an articulate voice for a generation of native-born Americans who sincerely wanted to incorporate newcomers into America. Barnum assembled the familiar Progressive building blocks of efficiency, industrial democracy, education, and corporatism into a popular ideology that included the notion of the working woman. She helped define the nature and institutions of American mainstream feminism and to position it with reference to the state and labor movement.

Barnum mysteriously disappeared from public view shortly after the passage of the Nineteenth Amendment, and we can only speculate on her reasons. Did she assume that female suffrage would resolve all social problems? Did her refusal to endorse protective legislation cut her off from her reform "home" in WTUL? Did the "nervous prostration" that forced her to withdraw from public life in 1897 return? Or was she weary of the fragmented and lonely life of the organizer? Whatever her reasons, her large Maybeck-style home still stands on Benvenue Street in Berkeley as testimony to the comfort of her retirement. Her 1945 letter to Fannia Cohn and the report that she was writing a history of the labor movement at the time of her death suggest that she remained interested in American workers. Her concern with questions of work, gender identity, and activist strategies, which were often played out in her fiction, created, without her knowledge, a paradigm that we can explore further in the lives of Mary Dreier, Pauline Newman, and Rose Pesotta.

2

Mary Dreier

1876–1963
"a guiding star"

In 1909, New York City police arrested Mary Dreier for picketing during a walk-out of garment workers at the Triangle Shirtwaist Factory. The *American Journal Examiner* called Dreier's arrest "utterly shameful." The arresting officer, too, expressed embarrassment: he would not have arrested Dreier had he known she was "the rich working girls' friend."[1] As president of the New York Women's Trade Union League, Dreier was indeed an ally of workers. But to the working girls she was far more than a wealthy benefactor. The *Journal Examiner* correctly saw Dreier's appearance before the judge as an act that "simply adds to the affection that the working girls feel for her."[2]

The affection was well placed. Dreier's arrest drew public attention to the physical and verbal abuse that strikers suffered at the hands of police. But in a more intangible way, the arrest of a prominent and respectable lady legitimated the strikers in the eyes of their families and neighbors. Dreier knew the social cost of the

strike to workers. As president of the New York Women's Trade Union League, she planned "all sorts of honors and appreciations for the girls to lessen the blows" of social dishonor, for, as she said, "it was a hard and sad thing for the mothers of some of these young girls as they thought of arrests as a terrible disgrace."[3]

Family, respectability, social decorum—it would be easy to dismiss Dreier's concerns as bourgeois and out of touch with the bread-and-butter needs of workers. But Dreier's sensitivity to the concerns of workers outside the workplace inspired Mary Goff, a garment worker and shop chairlady, to call her "a guiding star"[4] and prompted Pauline Newman to say, "She didn't carry a trade union card, but there was no more devoted trade unionist than Mary Dreier."[5] Of course, Dreier was neither a working girl nor a trade unionist, but neither was she simply the rich working girls' friend. Like Gertrude Barnum, Mary Elizabeth Dreier was a Progressive—a member of an army of reformers who waged war on the deleterious effects of industrial change in the United States between 1890 and 1915. Her roles as president of the New York Women's Trade Union League, vice president of the New York Women's City Club, and active suffragist put her in the vanguard of a unique female legion in the Progressive army, whose members included Jane Addams, Eleanor Roosevelt, Florence Kelley, Barnum, and a host of lesser-known women. Like some Progressives, but certainly not all, she came to support the New Deal, seeing the support of Roosevelt for the disadvantaged as an "encore for reform."

In her work with the Women's Trade Union League and in her writings, Dreier struggled to mediate between women of different classes. But Newman's remark notwithstanding, Dreier had little faith in what the labor movement could offer women. Early in her career she began pragmatically shifting from voluntarist to institutional to welfare-state solutions to the problems of working women. In part, she embraced these strategies in response to the entrenched sexism of the labor movement. Dreier, like many of her colleagues in the yeasty women's political culture of the turn of the century, believed that separate women's organizations were more effective than mixed-sex ones. She often seemed more comfortable with the values and language of nineteenth-century moral reformers than with rationalist Progressives. As strongly as any nineteenth-century reformer, she contended that women afforded a needed spiritual and moral presence in American political life that could express itself through the vote, the state, and coalition politics. Indeed, her own moral presence seemed evident in her striking appearance.

Mary Dreier's arresting blue eyes figure prominently in her contemporaries' memories of her. "China Blue" one observer called them; "cornflower blue" was the description given by another. Frances Perkins remembered how Dreier's appearance affected members of the Jacoby Investigating Commission:

> If a member of the commission indicated that something that was proposed to remedy a hazard to life was far too expensive and would ruin the real estate business Mary Dreier would open her eyes in Christian astonishment that an idea of that sort would be in anybody's mind. At once he began to explain or apologize, as did everybody else. Without doing it consciously, she put them on the defensive for all their evil and materialistic faults.

Perkins was quick to note that this behavior was utterly unselfconscious on Dreier's part and concluded that Dreier "had a great conscience, a very keen mind, understood everything, [and] learned the lessons very well indeed"—but Perkins concluded that in addition to these intellectual assets, Dreier "had this enormous moral influence with the commission."[6]

The second persistent memory shared by friends and associates of Mary Dreier was a temperament that evoked the appellation "Blessed Angel St. Mary" from her brother-in-law, Raymond Robins. Trade unionist Rose Schneiderman found her "a spiritual inspiration . . . patient, tolerant, totally devoted to the working woman's cause, and one of the most generous people" she had ever met. Schneiderman, her biographer tells us, "tried hard to be the saint that she thought Mary Dreier was."[7]

Her contemporaries' assessment of Mary Dreier threatens to give her life a hagiographic patina. However revered and adored she may have been, we should remember Frances Perkins's comment that Dreier was also "the most useful girl there ever was." Dreier's spirituality and her usefulness on the reform and labor scene allowed her to serve as a bridge between the moral imperatives of nineteenth-century feminism and the political strategies of white Protestant middle-class women after 1900.[8]

Mary Elizabeth Dreier, born in 1875, was the fourth of five children of Dorothea and Theodor Dreier, a wealthy Brooklyn couple. All three of her sisters had notable careers in reform and the arts, and her brother followed her father into business. When she is viewed in the context of her parents and her home, church, and community, Mary Dreier's choice of reform work seems almost inevitable. If she had been born several decades earlier, she would undoubtedly have spent much of her life doing charitable works, in line with family tradition. But Dreier came of age in an America strikingly aware of its acute social problems and among women interested in solving them. She found the tenets of the Social Gospel compatible with the ethic of Christian-inspired social responsibility that characterized her family.

Mary Dreier wrote two books. One, a biography of her sister Margaret Dreier Robins, was published in 1950. The other, an autobiographical novel written in 1914, remained unpublished; a publisher's rejection notice observed that public interest had ebbed in such tales of social reform. Both books are as telling about their author as about their subjects. Both are narratives constructed around an ideal of womanhood.

In *Margaret Dreier Robins*, the parents of the remarkable Dreier brood emerge almost as burghers—hopeful, rational, and prosperous. Theodor Dreier, a merchant, was born in Bremen. His wife, Dorothea, also German, was remembered by Mary as "beautiful . . . spontaneously gay with a contagious laugh." Together the parents created a "sheltered home" that "held security, beauty and culture." The children spent summers in a cottage crowded with lively groups of their friends. And summer days were filled with music, sketching, family picnics, and horseback riding. Little marred this domestic idyll. Mary spoke of "a happy family, unspoiled and ruled lovingly and understandingly by the parents." Beyond the immediate family circle, the Dreiers were close to their German relatives and visited Germany every two years for a few months while their grandparents were alive.[9]

Children in the Dreier home learned democratic and Christian values by word and example, according to Mary. Gossip was forbidden at the dinner table, and children were told to judge people on "qualities of heart and mind" rather than on wealth or status. After being widowed, Dorothea Dreier continued a lifetime tradition of service, establishing a home for rest and recreation for "mothers of children who needed time for themselves."[10]

Religion shaped Dreier's values, provided expression for her strongly spiritual nature, and, at least during her childhood, was an integral part of daily life. For the Dreiers, religion meant Sunday worship at Brooklyn's German Evangelical Church, morning Bible reading, and evenings spent singing Christian hymns.[11] As an adult, Dreier left the evangelicalism of her youth and converted to Presbyterianism, to which she may have been drawn by its liberal social agenda. Like her sister Katherine, she was fascinated by spiritualism.

Unlike Gertrude Barnum and other "New Women," she had no college experience—the Dreiers felt that colleges lacked a sufficiently humanistic curriculum and sent none of their children to college. Dreier was educated at the progressive George Brackett's School in Brooklyn Heights and spent a year at the New York School of Civics and Philanthropy. Alone among her siblings, Dreier resented not attending college.

Dreier's desire for higher education emerges in a thinly disguised unpublished autobiographical novel, "Barbara Richards."[12] The novel, despite its predictable moralism, provides important insights into Dreier's sense of herself, her view of femininity, and her notions of women's social purpose. It is at once a romance, a bildungsroman, and a social text.

Barbara Richards's story begins at the heroine's college graduation ceremony. Her "longing to be at one with the world, to find the purpose of her being," was inspired by the commencement speaker and his theme of industrial justice. Barbara's search for meaningful work led her to reject the relief work done by her mother for tuberculosis patients and choose instead to identify the environmental cause of social ills and eradicate them through education rather than welfare. The spunky Barbara questioned a social worker: "What was the cause of tuberculosis anyway? Why was it spoken of as an industrial disease? What were the conditions in industry that caused it? Bad air, bad conditions generally. *Why* was there bad air? Why shouldn't factories have good air?"[13]

Although, like the Dreier household, the Richards home "resounded with the laughter of young people" whose lives were animated by "rides and drives, picnics and dances, canoe trips down the river," Dreier also seemed to express unfulfilled wishes and a sense of separation or distance from her parents through Barbara Richards's persona. Barbara, unlike Mary, was an only child, and when her parents counseled her to marry and "create a home of [her] own," Barbara quickly replied, "how inadequate!" In Barbara's mind, as in the minds of most middle-class Americans, domestic female roles by definition excluded work in the public sphere.[14]

As Barbara proceeded with her plan to become an industrial reformer and an economically independent woman, she was deeply disappointed by her parents' lack of support and understanding. When Barbara's father opposed her move to a settlement house, Barbara "found herself growing hot from anger, and she broke forth passionately: "That's the trouble with you! I mean you men, all of you. You never believe we are in earnest, never believe we really care for ideals, for truth, for right, for nobility as much as for our bread and butter. And I believe just as long as we live off your earnings, whether as daughters or wives or what, that you will never believe that we love passionately honor and right more than the luxury you heap upon us."[15]

It is difficult to imagine this scene played out between the Blessed Angel St. Mary and her godly father! By the time Dreier began her career in reform, both of her parents had died, and she had clearly turned from their practice of philanthropy to an approach to social problems more in keeping with Progressive philosophy. If "Barbara Richards" is meant to be autobiographical, we must assume that Mary Dreier's full-time commitment to industrial reform and her rejection of marital domesticity broke with her parents' values and were implicated in her development of a separate, individual identity.

Barbara and Mary were as one in their religious motivation for reform: "I think it is the spirit of God in men, saying 'Barbara—find your place in the world, you must be and do'." Such religious sensibility pervaded Dreier's daily life and language. Many years after defining Barbara Richards's motives, for example, Dreier expressed support for Franklin Roosevelt and New Deal policies as the infusion of "our economic life with the spirit of God."[16]

Like Barnum's pigheaded girl, "Barbara Richards" uses a romantic trope to resolve some of the tensions of modernity for women. At first glance, Barbara Richards is the pigheaded girl with a name. Dreier's novel makes the same argument for the compatibility of work and marriage that appears in Barnum's more allegorical story. But a closer reading of both works reveals significant differences in the texts. The pigheaded girl was an orphan, raised by an aunt and uncle.[17] She made her way in the world influenced by experience and her own ingenuity. Barbara's college years developed her vision of the world, her Christian ideals motivated her commitment to reform work, and her decision to work ruptured her relationship with her family. In other words, where Barnum avoided the problem of generational conflict by making her heroine an orphan, Dreier met the problem head-on. Moreover, Barbara's angry outburst at her father allowed Dreier the radical move of criticizing patriarchal family arrangements and conventional sex roles. Women, she asserted, are capable of higher ideals that transcend domesticity.[18]

"Barbara Richards" offers a model of marriage as well as a critique of patriarchy. Her fiancé (first introduced to readers as Barbara's college commencement speaker) shares Barbara's goals of social justice and Christian ideals. When chance brings them together years later, he explains her attraction for him: "You seem to me made up wholly of spirit and flame—the spirit of democracy and the flame of enthusiasm." The novel included a physician who lectured a couple on the "biological" and "human side" of marriage, a device that allowed Dreier to portray sex—wholesome, heterosexual, and marital—as a key component of women's happiness and satisfaction.[19]

The model for companionate marriage—and Mary Dreier certainly created one in "Barbara Richards"—did not simply emerge from Dreier's imagination but drew on the marriage of her sister Margaret and Raymond Robins. Robins first met Mary's sister Margaret when he spoke to a Chicago audience on the Social Gospel. Margaret became one of a few professional women in the early twentieth century who continued her work after her marriage—a move made possible because her husband shared her ideals. The romantic conventions of "Barbara Richards" allowed Dreier to manipulate her characters' motivations and the source of their attraction for each other but demanded that the author end the story with marriage. The biographical conventions enabled Dreier to extend the story of a woman's life beyond the wedding but (at least in the 1950s when Dreier wrote the story of her sister's life) precluded discussion of the personal. The two texts when examined together enable us to construct Dreier's idealistic sense of the possibilities of a woman's life, fulfilled on a number of levels.

But of course Dreier constructed a third "text" of a woman's life—her own. Religion, the privilege created by wealth, and a deeply rooted sense of social justice—all shaped Dreier's early life as well as that of the fictional Barbara. Both needed only the message of the Social Gospel, the program of Christian responsibility for social problems, to fuse these elements into a lifelong commitment to social reform. But unlike Barnum and others whose awakening came with education and settlement-house work, Dreier embarked upon reform through the efforts of her mentors and with their support. The four most influential—and beloved—

figures in Mary Drier's life all shared her passionate concern for social justice. Each in his or her own way was a mentor, each a lifelong friend.

Leonora O'Reilly, an Irish immigrant and working woman, was head resident at Brooklyn's Asacog House when she met Mary and Margaret Dreier in 1899. The growing friendship between the sisters and O'Reilly led naturally in 1904 to O'Reilly's sponsorship of Mary and Margaret in the newly formed WTUL. O'Reilly's warmth, her working-class roots, and her uncompromising political beliefs made her a model for Dreier until O'Reilly's death in 1926. She gave O'Reilly a house and a life income in 1907; a year later she described their friendship as "a strange and beautiful mixture of personal and impersonal."[20] Their loving relationship mirrored the League at its best—an organization of middle- and working-class women whose shared goals transcended class boundaries.[21]

The other pillar of Mary Dreier's personal and professional life was her practical and confident older sister, Margaret. As national president of the League from 1907 to 1922, Margaret decisively shaped its agenda and principles.[22] Equally important, she contributed much of her considerable fortune to underwriting its activities. The voluminous correspondence between Margaret and Mary, who herself was president of the New York chapter between 1906 and 1914, describes the ideas and strategies that guided the organization during its most active years. The sisters sometimes disagreed about what was best for the League and the working girl, but they never wavered from their shared and passionate devotion to the cause of social justice.

The League was not Mary Dreier's only passion. Before her death, Dreier entrusted her nephew with two packets of letters, each tied with a pink ribbon, and asked that they be buried with her. Theodor Dreier did not comply with her request, and the letters found their way into her papers bound for the Schlesinger Library archives. The first set of letters had been sent to Dreier by Frances Kellor; the second by her brother-in-law, Raymond Robins.[23]

Dreier began in 1904 to share a home with Frances Kellor. Thus began a partnership that endured until Kellor's death in 1952. Like Dreier, Kellor was a prominent reformer, but in background, temperament, and personal style they were opposites. Unlike Dreier, Kellor had been born into poverty, had been raised by a single mother, and had supported herself through Cornell Law School and graduate school at the University of Chicago. When Dreier met her in 1904, Kellor had published *Experimental Sociology*, which linked environmental factors to problems of juvenile delinquency, unemployed women, and black migrants, and *Out to Work*, a study of employment agencies. She had been a resident at the College Settlement House and at Hull House. Educated, employed, and an activist, she was all that Mary Dreier wished to be. And where Dreier was traditionally feminine, Kellor had a brusque manner and a tailored appearance.

Dreier and Kellor probably met when both worked for the Inter-Municipal Committee on Household Research, an independent reform agency. Mary Dreier, a volunteer, headed the legislative committee of the organization, drafting proposals for remedial legislation concerning child labor, employment agencies, and tenement houses. Kellor, a professional staff member, was committed to presenting the cause of immigrants to legislators and government officials. Around 1915 she began to focus on Americanization programs designed to assimilate immigrants. But the work for which she is best remembered began in 1926 with her involvement in the American Arbitration Association and continued until her death in 1952. Convinced that arbitration was the best approach to industrial disputes as well as international ones, she published a code of ethics for arbitrators and served on the executive board of the Pan American Union.

As with any close and long-term relationship, it is difficult to assess the extent to which Kellor and Dreier influenced each other. Politically, both were progressives; Dreier, like Kellor, believed that reform was best achieved by investigation, analysis, and legislation. In fact, Dreier may have lost interest in the labor movement after 1914 at least partly because of Kellor's conviction that legislative reform was the most effective remedy for social ills. Dreier, it seems, never converted her friend to her religious way of looking at the world, although in the first flush of their romance, Kellor indulged her beloved by reading the Bible and pronounced it "poetic."[24]

To judge from her letters, Kellor was passionately in love with Mary Dreier and became or at least wanted to become her champion before a misunderstanding world. The women were "sixy" and "seven" in a correspondence that began as early as December 1904. "Sixy dear," Kellor wrote, "Your note was very dear and you are so precious. I do love my darling. Seven." Kellor often referred to Dreier as "little girl," "naughty little girl," "sweet little girl," and "spoiled."[25]

A lengthy letter written by Kellor commemorating their first anniversary leaves little doubt as to the passionate nature of their relationship: "You are such a frail little body that needs so much looking after—like some exquisitely beautiful flower—and that beautiful mind of yours which so depreciates itself and which so few have ever tried to help grow. When I think of the limitations you have known by the thoughtlessness of others, my heart grows sick and a great longing fills my soul to just gather you up . . . I am so unworthy to love you dear—you seem sometimes so beyond me. And when you talk about our growing together and that one may not keep up—or perhaps it be the silences of the night when you nestle close to me to be comforted and assured that you are not alone."[26]

With Kellor, Dreier was not the "little sister" that she was to Margaret or to her brother-in-law but a soulmate who seemed occasionally intimidating. Certainly, these words, coming from a distinguished attorney, must have flattered a woman who longed for higher education. Dreier's relationship with Kellor began around the time of her sister Margaret's marriage to fellow reformer Raymond Robins. Margaret told her younger sister that her marital situation was "without question the greatest honor to befall a woman . . . the greatest honor, the supreme joy, the fulfillment full of glory of my life. May it some day, dear come to you!" Despite her sister's wish, Mary's choice of a woman as a life companion was actually more conventional within their circle of reformers. "Boston marriages" were common and accepted among women with sufficient wealth to live without a husband's income.[27]

Despite her relationship with Kellor, Mary Dreier maintained particularly intimate ties with her brother-in-law Raymond Robins. Shared religious and sentimental sensibilities led them to form a fanciful "Order of the Flaming Cross" in which Raymond was "Knight" and Mary "Lady." Both Margaret's biographer Elizabeth Anne Payne and Raymond's biographer Neil Saltzman characterize the closeness between Mary and Raymond as "passion" and assume that Raymond "persuaded Mary to sacrifice her passion to the cause of reform."[28] The mysterious bundle of letters certainly suggests romantic, if not sexual, feelings on the part of Mary for her brother-in-law, but as Payne herself suggests, these feelings ebbed and flowed during a relationship that lasted almost fifty years, and although many opportunities must have presented themselves, they were probably never acted upon.

The bonds of love and friendship that tied her to Frances Kellor, Margaret Dreier Robins, Raymond Robins, and Leonora O'Reilly, as well as her daily experiences with the WTUL, helped Dreier by 1909 to feel assured and confident in her role in the reform movement. By that time, New York had the largest and most active of the League chapters. As president, Dreier brought money, commitment, and above all, as we have seen, a remarkable ability to inspire the trust of working women.

During her years as president of the New York Women's Trade Union League, Mary Dreier, like Barnum, hoped that the labor movement would bring industrial democracy to the workplace. Initially she believed that trade unions would usher in democracy by giving workers a "vote" in how work was organized and how workers were paid as well as by affording them recourse in labor disputes. The feudal system of industry would be displaced by a more just and equitable relationship, that of worker and manager.

Dreier's goal was, quite simply, to help the public accept as inevitable the presence of women in industry, to illuminate its potential, and to protect motherhood as represented by these women. She often said that women had been "forced to enter industry" but in the same breath stressed the "supreme importance for women to be independent, it gives them more dignity and more value as human beings." In other words, Dreier struggled to reconcile, on the one hand, the inevitable presence of women in industry with independence and, on the other independence with maternity. But in ways unrelated to the struggle, Dreier was committed to the notion that dignity and human worth were goals that could be achieved if women were paid decent wages and went into a clean safe workplace without fear of sexual harassment.

Dreier's more intangible goals were part of the League's program from the first. The organization's uniquely feminist attempt to join elite and working-class women in campaigns to organize women workers into trade unions and improve their work environment was a perfect vehicle for Dreier's sense of Christian social responsibility. But the organization actually met the needs of two groups of women—poor and unorganized women working in sweatshops or tenements and privileged women like the Dreier sisters who sought a focus for their intelligence, energy, and designs for social welfare.

The seal of the WTUL offers an important clue to its sense of mission. Against the background of a brilliantly rising sun and a smoking factory, two women shake hands. The soft rounded figure on the left holds an infant and contrasts sharply with the large-breasted heroic figure on the right, who holds a shield labeled "Victory." Nature and industry, madonna and amazon, these classic emblems of womanhood clasp hands atop the League's three stated goals: an eight-hour day, a living wage, and protection of the home.

Both the image and the text are of interest here. The feminized warrior with her symbols of power, a shield and armor appropriated from men, is, like Artemis, a protector of women. The vulnerable woman and child are threatened by the smoke and squalor of modern industry. Women of the League like Dreier clearly saw the empowered classical figure as embodying the social purpose of their work and deliberately juxtaposed it with the more commonly displayed maternal figure. The image promotes social acceptance for women's public influence if it is deployed in the service of the home.

Equally important is the legend below the image. Higher wages and shorter hours had been part of the labor movement's agenda since its beginnings, but the League's addition of home guardianship infused labor reform with nineteenth-century moral concerns. The League and its founders realized that, for women, home could never be separated from the workplace. Accordingly, they created a distinct agenda for women workers and reformers. When the labor movement proved unresponsive to the goals of home protection, the League developed new strategies to reach its goals.

Dreier herself often used maternalist rhetoric and home protection when she championed rights for working women. But she also cast her arguments in purely political terms rather than in maternalist rhetoric. Her editorials painted a picture of young immigrant women attracted to the United States by ideals of freedom but now held in industrial bondage. Dreier called on union women to bring the legacy of Lincoln to their unorganized sisters. "Lincoln, the emancipator, the bringer of liberty to the enslaved black brother—why not you, my trade union sister, the emancipator, the bringer of hope, the bringer of liberty to these enslaved sisters both black and white?"[29]

As Dreier enveloped the struggles of working women in the cloak of American history, she made a rhetorical attempt at Americanization, folding the ideals and activities of immigrant workers into a palpable liberal mold.[30] Like other popular Progressives, she used familiar language and images to enable middle-class readers to identify with workers. By linking workers to an image of Lincoln, she could help both middle-class and working-class readers see themselves as Americans and believe that their cause was just.

But Lincoln and history were abstractions. Dreier also demonstrated the shared interests of workers and middle-class consumers. Making the connection between the classes more immediate, Dreier wrote of striking neckwear workers who made fashionable ties. She sought to link the world of the "gorgeous puffy cravat and the wretched tenements and sweatshops where it was made." A successful strike for youthful and enthusiastic workers meant, not social disruption, but "the standardization of a trade . . . and the establishment of democracy in the workshop."[31] Like Barnum, her words resonated with the rationalism of progressives and the democratic ideals so dear to her heart.

In the League's early years, Dreier focused on establishing democracy in the "most exploited trades." Through organization, workers in garment factories, commercial laundries, and other "sweated trades" would achieve industrial democracy, which would then produce better hours, wages, and working conditions for female workers. And as technology continued to de-skill jobs, particularly those filled by women, an organized workplace would be more secure against layoffs.[32] Dreier and many of the other allies in the League initially saw trade unionism as the solution to the plight of women toiling in New York's sweatshops and tenements. But their concept of the trade union was a far cry from the bread-and-butter or business unionism of the American Federation of Labor.[33] Like Barnum and others who looked to Europe for models of industrial organization, Dreier envisioned the trade union as a welfare institution. She called the union "a sort of mothering institution" that would be both a model of democracy and a surrogate family protecting the health and morals of its female members.

Like Barnum and other WTUL allies, too, Mary Dreier believed that trade unions could and should accomplish far more than increasing workers' wages and reducing their hours. A better standard of living would rescue working women from delinquency, dance halls, and a "maze of vice" and would promote a much-needed sense of dignity and human worth. Union membership would protect the woman worker at the shop from "insults and other dangers." The benefits of trade unionism, then, were moral as well as material. Dreier lyrically described potential union members as "hundred of thousands of young girls, many of them untarnished, many of them in the beginning of moral and spiritual awakening, uncertain, sensing their way, dreaming dreams and seeing visions, in the bloom of their young womanhood." Dreier concluded, "Fathers and mothers can't protect them. . . . the state cannot. . . . only one protection is possible and that is the trade union."[34]

By 1914, it was clear that the male- and craft-dominated labor movement would not assume a parental role. The American Federation of Labor regarded unskilled workers and, by extension, women workers as impossible to organize and as threatening a stable labor market. But what Dreier hoped the labor movement would be, the League became. Dreier recalled members who preached "the gospel of trade unionism" on street corners like "Salvation Army lassies." She wrote nostalgically of a time "before unions were strong enough, [when] the League helped with the trade agreements, sat in on discussions between employers and their young workers, and sat with the girls in their meetings to teach the methods of organizing, etc." But then the WTUL began to take on the characteristics of a social welfare organization. "In every possible way the League sought to reach the girls—through educational opportunity in English classes, singing and voice culture, health talks and a cooperative health group that unfortunately did not hold together. Through publicity, meetings, speeches, social events, picnics—truly, no way of approach was neglected."[35]

Eventually, though, the state came to play a more prominent role in Dreier's reform schema than trade unions or League social events. As early as 1917, she cautioned that the state would lose a "vigorous, strong womanhood" if it failed to protect women. Disillusioned by the entrenched sexism of the labor movement, she adopted woman suffrage, investigating committees, electoral politics, and lobbying as her favored approaches to reform. Still, her arguments were often constructed to highlight the women's particular nature and needs. Like Barnum, she spoke with conviction of the contribution that working women could make to the suffrage movement and explained how the vote, once won, would be a powerful aid in improving the welfare of the female worker. In one address to a suffrage group, she pointed out that long hours at work precluded active involvement in the suffrage movement for most working women but that, for organized women, union activities were "their suffrage training." Union women, she wrote proudly, had begun street speaking five years ahead of the suffragists.

By 1918 she was building reform coalitions such as the Women's Joint Legislative Conference, consisting of the New York State Suffrage Party, the YWCA, the WTUL, the Consumer's League of New York State, and the Consumer's League of New York City, to support such proposals as the eight-hour day, the minimum wage, and health insurance and protection for office workers, transportation workers, and elevator operators.

Dreier's feminism animated all these endeavors. Her political perspective, though, rather than her ideology drew her to issues. Political candidates won her allegiance through their support for industrial reform rather than by their endorsement of the Right or the Left. She habitually crossed party lines and at various times joined the Progressive Party, voted for Republican Charles Evans Hughes, campaigned for Republican judges, joined the American Labor Party, and avidly supported Roosevelt's New Deal.[36]

Dreier deployed this pragmatic feminism on two interrelated fronts: with groups that involved only women and when she represented women's groups. Particularly in the busy decade between 1905 and 1915, her commitment to feminism always interacted dynamically, even opportunistically, with the politics of the times. If a political door opened, she stepped through it armed with moral conviction.

Her response to the Triangle Shirtwaist fire is particularly telling of this approach. Dreier was president of the NYWTUL at the time of the tragedy. The gruesome spectacle of 146 young girls plummeting to their death and the awful truth that the fire was caused by unsafe factory conditions galvanized the reform community. The League organized a funeral for the seven unidentified victims of the fire on 28 March 1911. The somber drama included "about one hundred thousand workers and representatives of all professions . . . In the rain, another four hundred thousand lined the streets. There were no banners and no music; only the sound of marching feet."[37]

Dreier was appointed to the Committee on Safety formed in the aftermath of the fire. The New York state legislature responded to pressure from the committee by approving in May the Wagner-Smith Resolution creating the New York State Factory Investigating Commission (FIC), whose members included Al Smith, the future governor of New York and presidential candidate, and Robert Wagner, later a senator from New York.[38]

Dreier's membership on the commission furthered her education in industrial labor conditions and refined her ideas about reform strategies. Between 1911 and 1915 Dreier joined other commission members in visits, often unannounced, to canneries, sweatshops, and tenements throughout New York state. She heard hundreds of hours of testimony on "sanitation, industrial disease, machinery, hours, workmen's compensation and wages . . . In one six month period [the commission] held 22 public hearings, examined witnesses, published 1986 pages of testimony and met in 15 executive sessions to formulate recommendations."[39] We can readily understand Dreier's lifelong support for protective legislation when we read her description of the pea cannery, where women and children worked long hours, "picking out foreign particles from the peas as they swept by on a belt." The work "caused eye strain, especially at night when the only lighting was a few bare bulbs hanging from the ceiling, and the steady stream of peas on the moving belt often produced a nausea akin to seasickness."[40]

The commission was immensely successful. Like Dreier, it took the position that the minimum wage was critical to the welfare of women workers. By 1913, the state legislature had passed eight of fifteen bills recommended by the group, and it passed twenty-six of twenty-eight the following year. By the time the commission had completed its work, it had "conducted the most intensive study of industry undertaken in the United States until that time."[41]

As Dreier eagerly participated in the work of the Factory Investigating Commission, she expanded her community of politically aware women beyond the NYWTUL. Early in 1916, she became vice president of the newly formed New York Women's City Club, which was founded on the model of men's clubs to create a place where women could "study and debate political issues." She and other prominent Progressives like Belle Moskowitz, Ida Tarbell, Mary Simkhovitch, Frances Perkins, and Eleanor Roosevelt met in the club's suite of rooms on the top floor of the Vanderbilt Hotel (in 1920 the group moved to an elegant mansion at Thirty-fifth and Park).[42]

The members of the New York Women's City Club reinforced Dreier's ideas about women's political effectiveness and the need for separate women's organizations. In 1916, Dreier made a decisive break with trade union politics. Writing to Leonora O'Reilly, she noted, "The enfranchisement of all women is the paramount issue for me. . . . the attitude of the labor men to the working women has changed me from being an ardent supporter of labor to a somewhat rabid supporter of women and to feel that the enfranchisement of women and especially my working sisters is the supreme issue."[43]

What specifically inspired Dreier's switch of allegiance from trade union organizing to suffrage? Was it her experience on the all-male FIC? Certainly AFL president Samuel Gompers amply demonstrated his indifference toward unskilled and female workers during his tenure on the commission.[44] Or was she, like so many of her sister allies in the WTUL, frustrated at being obliged to lobby in Albany and Washington as an unenfranchised citizen? Many League members had begun even by 1913 to see the strategic links between the vote and the industrial conditions they so earnestly sought to ameliorate.[45] Whatever her rationale, by 1916, Dreier had become so committed to suffrage that she supported the antilabor, prosuffrage Charles Evans Hughes for president rather than Wilson.

As Dreier shifted her strategies, so too did the League shift its emphasis to suffrage and protective legislation in the years after 1913.[46] Some historians blame the WTUL's failure to organize women on that shift, for it "left the work of unionizing women to uninterested men."[47] Such statements of course reflect historical hindsight. "Failure" was not apparent to Mary Dreier in the years of peak agitation for suffrage. For her the vote meant that women would be taken seriously in the workplace, in collective bargaining situations, and before the legislature. Once enfranchised, women could exercise significant support of industrial reform at the ballot box. And Dreier believed that working women could be equal partners with the middle class in suffrage just as they had been in the League.

Dreier, of course, faced the same predicament that confronted Barnum and other elite women eager to bring workers into the suffrage fold. An enlarged membership of working-class women would significantly alter the political balance of power in the movement and there was no guarantee that once working-class women had joined the movement, they would be content to follow rather than to lead.

Undeterred by this potential problem, League allies figured prominently in each of the three organizations formed between 1907 and 1916 to recruit working women. In 1907, Harriet Stanton Blatch left the League to form the Equality League for Self-Supporting Women.[48] In 1912, the WTUL organized the Wage Earner's Suffrage League, which admitted only working women as members. Finally, in 1914, Mary Dreier resigned as NYWTUL president to chair the Industrial Section of the Women Suffrage Party. Soon the League began to administer the Industrial Section and contributed experience in organizing street meetings in working-class neighborhoods and speaking at union meetings. The WTUL translated suffrage leaflets into Yiddish,

Italian, and German and sponsored a series of pamphlets addressed to working men and union members.[49] All these efforts were aimed at making suffrage as meaningful to the working, often immigrant, women and men of New York as to more elite women. Despite the efforts of all three groups, however, the 1915 referendum for female suffrage failed to pass in New York.[50]

The vigorous attempts to gain working-class support for suffrage never eliminated the movement's historical association with temperance and the upper classes. Two years later, however, after the defeat of the referendum in New York, a shift in political climate and the support of Tammany Hall, the Democratic "machine," resulted in an "easy" victory for the suffrage cause.[51]

Dreier was elated at the suffrage victory in New York. She agreed with Harriet Stanton Blatch that a "republican faith" could be applied to modern class relations. Like Blatch, she "believed that educational and professional achievement, rather than wealth and refinement, fitted a woman for social leadership."[52] In other words, women of noble and humble birth could compete in a kind of moral meritocracy that would ensure women's full participation as citizens. And true to her belief, Dreier readily supported such trade unionists as Rose Schneiderman and Pauline Newman for leadership positions in the League.

The same philosophy continued to inspire Mary Dreier even after the vote was won. Her activities belie the assertion that feminism died after the passage of suffrage. Elated by New York's approval of the suffrage referendum in 1917, Dreier brought four women's reform organizations into the Women's Joint Legislative Conference in 1918 with the hope of harnessing the untapped power of women's vote for the cause of social reform. The group was specifically to "lobby for social welfare laws and support women candidates for office."[53] The inference seems clear: women, regardless of their party affiliation, could be counted upon to back reform.

The conference's first opportunity to achieve its goal soon came. It succeeded in passing a bill in the New York state legislature to protect elevator and transportation workers but faced a formidable foe in the speaker of the New York General Assembly, Thaddeus Sweet. Sweet, a paper mill owner and chairman of the Rules Committee, frequently used his position to block reform legislation from the floor. The Women's Joint Legislative Conference, now armed with the franchise, decided to meet Sweet on his own ground and defeat him as representative from Oswego County. The conference drafted Marion Dickerman to run against Sweet, and Mary Dreier became her unofficial campaign manager. Coached by Dreier, Dickerman ran on a feminist platform that echoed the concerns of the WTUL: "a living wage for women and children in industry; an eight-hour day for women and children in factories and mercantile establishments; and equal pay for equal work." Dickerman joined these demands with planks aimed directly at the economic concerns of rural Oswego County.[54]

At first the farmers and villagers of Oswego County saw the downstate feminists as little more than a curiosity. Local newspapers scoffed: "Democratic Women Take Little Stock in Miss Dickerman" and "Real Working Women Opposed to So-Called Welfare Bills." Slowly, however, Dickerman rallies began attracting larger and more enthusiastic crowds. Reformers poured into Oswego County to aid the Dickerman campaign. Sweet's supporters worried about outside agitators and labeled Mary Dreier "a socialist and a Bolshevick." (Years later Dickerman wryly commented that while Mary Dreier was being called a Red in central New York state, she was hailed for having participated as a member of the women's committee in the election of Miss Bertha Rembaugh, a Republican, to the office of justice of a municipal court in New York City.)

The campaign invigorated political discourse in the rural districts of Oswego County. "Never in [their] history . . . had political matters attracted such interest. All records were broken, large halls . . . were packed to the doors with members of all political beliefs listening thoughtfully." Although Sweet won the election (17,000 votes to 10,000), his power was effectively challenged, and the campaign had publicized ideas about the state and social welfare outside urban areas.[55]

The Dickerman-Sweet election well illustrates Dreier's vision of suffrage. The vote was a means to an end. Once it had been attained, the task was to mobilize women in support of the type of reform agenda that had been proposed in Oswego County. Unfortunately, we have no gender breakdown of the vote in Oswego County, nor do we know how many women supported the welfare cause and responded to a female candidate. Still, the solidarity of the woman reformers is clear.[56] Dreier's feminism enabled her to cross boundaries of partisan politics. What mattered in this election was not that Thaddeus Sweet was a Republican and Marion Dickerman was a Democrat (or that Wilson was a Democrat and Hughes a Republican) but rather that there was a set of important social issues demanding party support.

Many historians have described the 1920s as hostile to social reform and feminism. But some have written about the "networks" of "friendship and cooperation" that included women like Dreier and Dickerman and see the relationships forged in them as laying the groundwork for women's participation in the New Deal.[57] Events such as the Dickerman-Sweet election, which mobilized reform-minded women, kept feminist activism alive during the 1920s. In part the women may have been able to persist because few faced personal demands of marriage and family. The boundaries between their public and private lives were highly permeable. The cohort of women whom Dreier once called "The Children of Light" were bound together by a shared history in suffrage and Progressive reform, by a sense of themselves as the first American women to enter public life, and by the ideology of feminism and the conception of a nascent welfare state. These women "thought of themselves as part of a large family bound together by an almost mystical commitment to social reform."[58]

The ideas and strategies of Dreier and her colleagues, though, were not obsolete remnants of a presuffrage past. Dreier, in particular, was interested in what Americans could learn from Europe. After World War I, she went abroad and later reported on industrial conditions in Belgium for *Life and Labor*. Her particular concern was relief workshops for women.[59] She brought German labor leader Karl Legien to speak to the NYWTUL and wrote approvingly of German social welfare policies such as the "out of work" benefit. Perhaps voicing her own disappointment with U.S. labor, she concluded, "It is in their well-laid plans for education and a wider vision that the German workers seem so far ahead of us."[60]

In December 1919, the WTUL hosted an International Congress of Working Women. Women from twelve countries assembled in Washington, D.C., to consider and endorse a program of protective legislation to be brought before the Labor Congress of the League of Nations. In 1921, the International Federation of Working Women was founded at a second international congress in Geneva. And in 1923, Dreier accompanied her sister Margaret to the third Working Women's International Congress in Vienna.[61] Their goal—hopeful then, frustrating now—was to realize the transnational potential of feminism. Part of the strong yet minority belief in internationalism following the First World War led the two sisters to believe that women's shared concerns—workplace equity and family protection—could bring women together in an influential bloc.

In 1926, Mary Dreier, like many a weary urbanite, complained, "I am sitting in this horrid city. It is so crowded there is hardly room to walk in the streets. It has never been so unpleasant."[62] To remedy her malaise, Dreier purchase a summer home overlooking the ocean in South West Harbor, Maine. Christened Valour House, it became a favorite spot for reformers to gather and also for the lively and extensive Dreier clan.

When Dreier was in New York during the 1920s, she continued to meet with reform-minded women at New York's Women's City Club. By the 1920s, the club, resplendent in its new headquarters at Thirty-fifth and Park, had shifted its attention from suffrage to an array of topical political issues. The club always took a reformist perspective, though, and the nonpartisan membership supported educational, lobbying, and legislative efforts on behalf of urban housing, the reorganization of state government, protective legislation, and the legalization of birth control. The club served as a political tutor for Eleanor Roosevelt during the 1920s, as it did for many other members. The future First Lady was elected to the board of directors in 1924 and became the club's first vice president the following year.[63]

Mary Dreier's life bridged the distance between the end of the first wave of feminism and the beginning of the second. Together with other social reformers, she was responsible for what historian Paula Baker has called "the domestication of politics," the way in which "social policy—formerly the province of women's voluntary work—became public policy."[64] While Baker sees this development as having sounded the death knell of separate women's and men's political cultures, Mary Dreier's activities from the 1920s through the 1950s attest to the persistence of women's political culture through a distinctive ideology as well as through organizations like the WTUL and the Women's City Club.

From the 1920s through the 1950s, many women who had been active in settlement work, in the suffrage movement, or in other areas of Progressive reform found themselves appointed to such government agencies as the Women's Bureau or being named educational directors of unions. While Dreier's wealth allowed her the luxury of continued affiliation with voluntary organizations, she corresponded with many of the women whom she had known during her years of activity in the League.

If anything, the women's political culture in which Dreier participated during the 1920s was modified rather than subsumed into the mainstream. The national WTUL convention in 1922, for example, reflected a broad liberal agenda. In addition to predictable resolutions concerning women and trade unions and "public service through government," there were resolutions "dealing with peace, outlawing of war, amnesty for political prisoners; against racial discrimination and a protest against the imprisonment of and death penalty for Sacco and Vanzetti." The indisputable moral force behind that agenda had not changed, however: "To set free the spirit of God within us."[65]

When economic collapse precipitated the election of Franklin Roosevelt in 1932, many reformers became eager recruits for his New Deal army. Roosevelt drew many of Dreier's Progressive friends and colleagues into government agencies; the new First Lady took feminist ideas into the administration. Frances Kellor exercised influence in the new administration through her approval of New Deal economic planning. Dreier confronted the massive social problems of the 1930s using the WTUL as her base.

Although Franklin Roosevelt stood high in Dreier's personal pantheon, the 1930s actually extended her public life in the teens and 1920s rather than bringing a new approach to social issues. Blessed Angel St. Mary responded to the pressing problems of unemployed women through WTUL programs. In 1931, the League appointed Dreier to chair a special committee established to work on relief proposals. She immediately set up rooms in the organization's headquarters to interview and advise unemployed women. Later the League opened a lunchroom where weary women looking for work could rest and have a hot meal.[66]

When League president Rose Schneiderman accepted a government position, Mary Dreier stepped in to become acting president. Between 1933 and 1935, as a spokesperson for women's issues, she campaigned vigorously on behalf of New Deal programs. In 1933, during a trip to six upstate New York cities, she spoke to various groups in support of unemployment insurance. While noting labor's enthusiasm for the measure and the "lip service" that many employers had paid to unemployment insurance legislation, she was careful to note separately that women had supported the measure. In her mind, women were a distinct political constituency and, in this case, one with specific interests that would be served by unemployment insurance.[67]

Despite Dreier's devotion to the Roosevelts and the New Deal ethos, her politics remained resolutely nonpartisan. In a 1937 radio address, she endorsed the American Labor Party and its platform of better housing for workers, public ownership of utilities and subways, a municipal distribution plant for milk, and more parks and playgrounds.[68]

Although the New Deal institutionalized programs and ideas that Dreier believed in, her public life still centered on an extensive network of women and organizations concerned with social justice and working women. During an era that saw the plight of the male industrial worker as emblematic of national problems, Dreier maintained a feminist concern for women's welfare. She continued to feel that feminism offered the woman worker greater hope than the labor movement. In 1938 she voiced her suspicions of labor when the post of New York commissioner of labor became vacant. As the network of women reformers mobilized to support Frieda Miller, Dreier commented to Miller that perhaps labor already had a candidate in mind, and she speculated wryly on "what the attitude of our Brethern would be if we rush you instead of helping them".[69]

In 1938, the attitude of Dreier's trade union "Brethern" continued to be benign indifference to working women. But while only a fraction of working women were unionized, those women who had been associated with the WTUL assumed many middle-level positions in certain unions. There they mobilized support for feminist issues and candidates.[70] The hundreds of letters that these women exchanged show that there was a highly interconnected network of trade union women, government officials, and women in voluntary organizations.[71]

For Dreier and her WTUL colleagues, feminism in the intrawar years also came to mean an implacable opposition to the Equal Rights Amendment. Time and again they marshaled their resources to lobby against passage of a proposal that would, they felt, erode the legislative gains for women that had been made during the Progressive period. Specifically, they worried that a constitutional guarantee of equal protection for women would undermine the protective legislation for which they had fought so hard.[72]

The ERA created a deep fissure among American feminists. The Women's Party, along with professional women's organizations and eventually the Business and Professional Women's Clubs, supported the proposal. The WTUL, the labor movement, and an array of women's organizations repeatedly rallied to defeat it, calling the ERA "a lunatic proposal" and the Women's Party the "ladies' auxiliary of the National Manufacturer's Association."[73]

Dreier and her associates saw firm opposition to the ERA as a feminist stance; the Women's Party saw its support for the amendment in the same light. The former group staunchly believed that the needs of the working woman (usually perceived as an industrial woman rather than a professional one) would be better served by protective legislation than by the ERA.

As vice president of the WTUL, Dreier adamantly opposed the ERA, and like other members, she advocated continued support of social reform legislation as the best solution to working women's problems. Even following World War II, Dreier and her colleagues urged the major political parties to adopt a plank addressing postwar employment for women as well as a proposal for a broader federal Social Security system. Expansion of the protective government umbrella, and not contraction, was needed to secure the gains women had made during the war years.

On the one hand, Dreier was quite right: labor, as always, had little interest in the women whom trade unions had organized during the war years. Trade unions, and the rest of the country, eagerly turned their attention to the welfare of the male veterans. By continuing to support the strategy of protection with a language of gender, however, Dreier and others differentiated the cause of the woman worker from that of men and reinforced stereotypes of women as weak and inherently domestic. Dreier's idealistic and often contradictory ideas about women in the twentieth century are well summarized in a letter that she wrote to Elisabeth Christman in 1944. While Dreier was in residence at Margaret and Raymond Robin's estate at Chinsegut Hill, Florida, she found time to reflect on the League and woman's place in post–World War II America. She endorsed women's right to work after the war with the same claim to seniority and equal pay as men. But with language rooted in another generation's experience, she added that women's right to work should not extend to situations that would jeopardize "the function of women as child bearers." In emphasizing women's biological role as mothers rather than their social role, she echoed the thought of Charlotte Perkins Gilman, another farsighted feminist Progressive, by urging "fantastic" proposals to incorporate the needs of working women into postwar housing plans. "These homes should be built with the clear understanding that women cannot be relegated to kitchen and house." Like Gilman, she envisioned apartments that would have public playrooms, laundries, and kitchens. Like Gilman, too, Dreier still saw the staffing of these facilities as women's work. Dreier advocated "leisure so that they will have more chance to become better citizens." She suggested as well the possibility of a "social settlement" in the tenements in which women could work "under supervision," and she made the "fantastic" suggestion that a GI Bill of Rights should be passed for industrial women.[74]

Dreier was well aware that her proposals might not find support among her labor colleagues. She cautioned Christman against having a foreward to the report written by AFL leaders Green and Murray "unless they accept our viewpoint." As she wrote, "Supposing they said women shd. be home and take care of the children who had to be so neglected during the war."[75]

The curious contradictions of Dreier's feminism are all apparent in this letter. There is no doubt that she was committed to maintaining and supporting women in industrial jobs. But her language stressed women's domestic roles as mothers and housekeepers. Her wariness of male labor leaders was as acute in 1944 as it had been thirty years earlier, and so was her obvious conviction that voluntarist organizations like the League better protected the interests of the female industrial worker than the labor movement did. But these organizations had seen their day, and as Dreier must have known, national and state welfare programs had adopted their ideas and many of their reform schemes.

By the late 1940s, the League was on the wane. Its remaining leaders were women in their sixties and seventies, the welfare state had largely accomplished its program of social reform, and contemporary trade unions regarded it as anachronistic.[76] Pauline Newman, writing to Mary Dreier in 1951, sadly commented, "Frankly, Mary, I don't think it will last long. It is not only the lack of money, but there does not seem to be a plan or a program of interest." She went on to discuss several officers who would probably quit and concluded with a wry comment on their annual meeting: "holding a conference once a year is not enough reason to keep an organization going, is it?"[77] Newman's prediction proved true. The League disbanded in 1953. Elisabeth Christman, the secretary-treasurer, briskly announced to the *New York Times* that the organization "had closed its boxes with the notation 'mission accomplished.' "[78]

At the time of the WTUL's demise, Dreier was deeply involved in another mission, writing the biography of her sister Margaret, who had died in 1945. It was, of course Dreier's second biography, and like the fictional "Barbara Richards," which she wrote at the beginning of her career, her story of her sister's life had strong elements of autobiography. *Margaret Dreier Robins: Her Life, Letters, and Work* was largely excerpted from the extensive correspondence that Robins had carried on with her sister and with other activists. It is a generous and uncritical portrait. Her sister, she believed had shared her moral conception of women's political culture and saw little difference between feminism and social reform. The biography linked them much as history has—as sisters to each other and to the thousands of women whom they hoped to serve.

Mary Dreier faced the last decade of her life without her most stalwart supporters. Leonora O'Reilly was long dead, and both Margaret and Frances Kellor had died. Raymond, crippled and increasingly rigid and dogmatic in his political views, finally died in 1954. These losses dimmed neither Dreier's spirit nor her interest in the world around her. She continued to correspond with old friends from the WTUL and to take pleasure in the extended

Dreier family. She spent ever longer periods of time at her beloved Valour House and became ever more deeply immersed in the history and natural setting of the rugged Maine coast. There, in a rare pensive mood, she wrote to Rose Schneidermann shortly before her death, "The tragedy of our human race seems to be overwhelming to me at times. How strange it is that people in various parts of the world should be so fearful that they would rather kill than even attempt friendship or understanding or tolerance. . . . we must admit that we are far from Christians when we develop hate and fear rather than love and tolerance."[79]

Dreier's words remind us that Christian ethics and values have permeated American reform even into the modern age. A sense of Christian social responsibility fueled Mary Dreier's feminism and her liberalism. Her sense of shared humanity blinded her to class conflict, but because she believed in the moral superiority of women, it also supported her feminism. With historical hindsight we can see that the program of protective legislation and separate organizations for women had its limitations. For Dreier, however, it appeared to be the most effective way to achieve a more ordered and ethical society.

3

Pauline Newman

c. 1888–1986

"a voice of the less articulate"

Pauline Newman—immigrant, Jew, socialist, worker—spent most of her adult life in the company of reformers like Gertrude Barnum and Mary Dreier. She shared their vision of a better life for working women and, like them, supported a feminist agenda that included suffrage and protective legislation. But Newman reached her community and her politics by a route far different from that of either Barnum or Dreier. Her life story involves assimilation of a very particular kind, a process that tempered "Americanization" with her ethnic and work experience and a feminism that synthesized a class and gender analysis of social problems. She later believed that it was her life's mission to be "the voice of the less articulate young men and women with whom I worked and with whom later I was to join in the fight for improved working conditions and a better life for us all."[1]

As Newman came to speak for the less articulate, she developed a language that bridged the Old World traditions of her

youth and the realities of her life in modern America. She mastered English, became a union organizer and union bureaucrat, read extensively, and wrote essays, poetry, and some fiction. In 1921, two decades after her arrival in the United States, she described her "credentials" for readers of the WTUL journal *Life and Labor*:

> I started life in the College of the Triangle Waist Company . . . at the age of 13. I graduated from there with honors, and proceded at once to the University of the Reliance Waist Company. Took several courses in similar institutions. Got my M.A. from the Ladies' Garment Workers' Union when I delivered an oration on "Shall we submit to the exploitation of Dean Low Wages and Professor Long Hours, or shall we organize in a school of our own?" With this diploma I toured for the I.L.G.W.U. for many years. . . . My post graduate work I took in the University of a cotton mill in Wauregan, Conn. Got my Ph.D. from the Women's Trade Union League of New York. Having been very desirous of obtaining a Doctor's degree for it means a great deal these days; it establishes a status for one without much difficulty—I began work with the Joint Board of Sanitary Control as inspector as well as lecturer and publicity agent.[2]

Written with characteristic good humor, and a sly poke at academic degrees, Newman's statement clearly expresses her ambivalence about formal education and her awareness of her own social mobility. As deeply as she prized books and ideas, she recognized the value of her own experience.

Newman's story began about twenty years before her "matriculation" at the Triangle Shirtwaist Company. Newman was born in Popelan, a small Lithuanian village, about 1888. She remembered a happy childhood until the death in 1900 of her beloved father.[3] A fruit vendor, he had broken with tradition by imparting to a girl the mysteries of the Talmud. Within a year, a brother in America sent for Pauline, her mother, and two sisters.[4] Like countless other immigrants, they packed up household goods and family treasures and departed on an arduous journey into the unknown.[5]

Like all "greenhorns," Newman was awestruck by the size and

energy of New York City. "There were always such crowds of people! People walking, standing, pushed each other; arguing, shouting drinking soda water at one cent a glass. . . . There were men speaking from soap boxes. . . . There was the Salvation Army with music and song and of course, the ever present push carts."[6]

But "the ugly tenements, the poverty, the squalor" cast a shadow over the bright new world, and Newman quickly encountered the dark underside of the New World's prosperity in the city's Lower East side sweatshops. Her work experience in the years between 1900 and 1909 reads like a primer in industrial conditions for women. The Yiddish sign "young girls wanted, no experience necessary" brought her to her first job, weighing hair in a hairbrush factory. The work was dirty, the hours long, and the wages characteristically low. When the brush factory closed, Newman took a job rolling cigarettes. Laid off after two weeks because the factory became overstocked, she entered the garment trades.

Newman first began work in an old walk-up, sewing buttons on shirtwaists. She longed to join the children she could see playing in the park across the street from the factory. Later she worked at the infamous Triangle Shirtwaist Company with children, who were used as "cleaners" to cut threads on finished garments. Inspectors who came to enforce child labor laws were always able to issue Triangle a clean bill of health, since the children were taught to scurry into rag-covered boxes when an inspection was in progress. Newman reached the factory after a long trolley car ride and was always conscious of the fine levied on workers who were even five minutes late. Once at the shop the women were watched constantly. Even lavatory visits were timed. The twelve-hour day ended at six o'clock unless there was overtime work, which was common. Yet Newman earned $1.50 per week and feared losing her job at Triangle. It was an era of surplus labor and no unemployment insurance.

These experiences taught Newman lessons—that male bosses had power, that capitalism begot injustice and inequity, and that the health and welfare of workers were profoundly affected by workshop conditions. In later years, Newman's effectiveness as an organizer and union official rested in part on her intimate knowledge of the shop scene: workers knew that she had endured their day-to-day routine. In spite of, or perhaps because of, the fatigue and tedium of work, she sought education to transcend and understand her immediate experience. She avidly read the "labor poets," who wrote in the labor and ethnic press. She decided to learn English and bought an English edition of *Great Expectations* from a pushcart vendor.

New York's Socialist Literary Society (SLS) offered her and many other young workers an incubus for learning and an education in socialism. At the SLS rooms Newman heard Eugene Debs, Jack London, Gaylord Wilshire, Meyer London, and Morris Hillquist discuss social transformation, the workers' plight, and the possibility, even the inevitability, of a socialist utopia. Although the SLS reserved full membership for male workers and American college men, allowing women only to attend lectures and classes, its rooms soon became home to Newman. In that formative time and place "my world of ideas and ideals began to take shape. Reading became my chief occupation (outside my work)." Years later, recalling the politics that attracted her to socialism, she spoke of the "vision, that we, the socialists, the people, all people, would have a chance to live in decency. We had a vision that justice and freedom and everything else we desired would be there under socialism and that your job was to bring it about and you did what you could."[7] Socialism offered an ideology that interpreted the world around her as well as a plan of action. Most important, it promised the average working woman and man a dignity that most found elusive in industrial America.

As her socialist education grew, Newman became active in the American Socialist Party. Socialism, particularly the pragmatic American variety, with its emphasis on immediate social goals rather than dogma, provided a focus for the emerging values of the adolescent girl. Newman's ideas and her later activity in the party brought about a rupture between her and her family. In an effort to wean her from socialist literature, her brother offered to send her to college. Newman refused to abandon the newspapers she found so meaningful and gradually created a surrogate family from like-minded friends. During a period of unemployment, she camped out with her friends on the Palisades and argued the issues of the day over pie and coffee in Child's restaurant. New York offered her both pleasure and problems, as it did Mary Dreier, but the refined world of Brooklyn Heights that Dreier knew seemed a long distance from Newman's Lower East Side. Newman's moral sensibilities reflected her experience of abysmal conditions in tenements and sweatshops that she knew "weren't right." Her reading of the *Jewish Daily Forward* and Dickens, and her participation in the SLS, gave her the language she needed to express her sense of injustice. Books and lectures led Newman to a socialist analysis of the problems of sweatshops and poverty. Capitalism's drive toward profit led to the exploitation and immiserization of workers; unions and electoral politics would empower the masses. Newman found the conflicting demands of class and gender less troubling during her early activist years than they would later become. Women, in the socialist lexicon, were workers and, by joining working men in unions and in the Socialist Party, would improve their lot. Collective action, in other words, could give power to the powerless.

Newman's growing role in movement culture gave her a confidence beyond her years and proved, at least in a superficial way, that activism reinforced femininity. She danced with Wobbly leader "Big Bill" Haywood at a Socialist ball at the Grand Central Palace, rode the "Red Special" campaign train with Gene Debs, and ran for various state offices (county clerk, sheriff, secretary of state) on the Socialist Party ticket. In 1907, she organized a rent strike; the newspaper headline read, "Chic Girl Leads Rent Strike."[8]

Newman came of age as an activist during a time of heady political and intellectual excitement. One event, however, stood out in her memory. Her first article, a simple description of neighborhood life, was published in the *Forward* and led her to be hailed by fellow workers as a "conquering hero." The experience prompted her to see with great clarity that it would be her life's mission to speak on behalf of her comrades in the shops and her neighbors on the Lower East Side.[9] Despite interests that increasingly drew her away from the sweatshop, Newman never lost her deep respect for the people she represented. She always maintained that the native intelligence of "her people" made them more effective organizers than better educated Americans.[10]

In 1909, the Uprising of the 20,000 shook Newman's life loose from its Lower East Side moorings and allowed her to pursue her developing commitment to social justice on a larger and more public stage.[10] As female workers walked off the job en masse for the first time in U.S. history, the general secretary of the International Ladies' Garment Workers' Union invited Newman to spearhead a fund-raising drive throughout New York state to support the strike. It was the first such assignment of many for Newman.

During the next four years, Newman crisscrossed fourteen states, speaking and organizing for the ILGWU, the Socialist Party, and the Women's Trade Union League. In her audiences she saw the varied face of labor and the extremes of class in America. Newman also developed a readership for the articles she published in the reform and labor press. In line with her organizational allegiances, she regularly wrote columns for the *Ladies' Garment Worker*, the *Progressive Woman*, and *Life and Labor*— papers of the ILGWU, the Socialist Party, and the WTUL, respectively. Increasingly her writings focused on the plight of the woman worker and reflected her experience as an organizer in several important strikes.

No event affected Newman more deeply than the Triangle Shirtwaist fire. It appeared as a leitmotif in her speeches and writings throughout her life. She returned to the tragedy again and again as the baseline against which to measure the accomplishments of reformers like herself. She repeatedly asked whether working conditions had been made sufficiently safe that such a disaster would never happen again. Six years after the fire, a labor paper published Newman's sentimental but heartfelt tribute to the victims:

They shall not grow old as we that are left grow old:
Age shall not weary them, nor years condemn.
At the going down of the sun and in the morning
We will remember them.[11]

Newman was in Philadelphia on 25 March 1911 when she received the news of the carnage. Shocked, she immediately took a train back to New York to share in the general outrage at the tragedy. Familiarity sharpened Newman's grief. She had worked eight years at Triangle and had many friends among the victims. For her, as for many other activists, the Triangle fire became a potent symbol, a defining moment to be remembered, with a eulogy for the victims, whenever working women gathered.[12] In the immediate aftermath, reformers like Mary Dreier began to investigate the unsafe and unsanitary factory conditions that had preceded the catastrophe. Newman, the quintessential organizer, was soon back on the road.

In June she joined Josephine Casey, a fellow ILGWU organizer, in an uprising of garment workers in Cleveland. Cleveland was not New York, though. The cross-class alliances that had led to the success of the great New York strikes failed to gel in Cleveland.[13] Despite such innovative techniques as special meetings for strikers' mothers, one historian tells us, "Casey and Newman were first and foremost working-class, union organizers, and they could not lend the needed air of respectability to strikers in general nor to women strikers in particular."[14] While Mary Dreier, "the working girls' rich friend," could cloak workers in respectability by her very presence, Newman's thick Yiddish accent would brand her as an immigrant if her plain shirtwaist did not.

But "respectability" was not, at least in 1912, Newman's concern. After the disappointing conclusion of the Cleveland uprising, she moved on to Kalamazoo, Michigan, where she urged striking corset workers to take an aggressive stance. Her strategy contrasted sharply with that of Josephine Casey and Gertrude

Barnum, the organizers she had been sent to replace. During the first three months of the strike, Casey eschewed violence and stressed issues of sexual harassment and unsanitary workshop conditions. By endorsing ladylike behavior and highlighting women's vulnerability, Casey hoped to elicit support from middle-class women.[15] She was jailed for defying an injunction in May and was replaced by Gertrude Barnum, who continued Casey's approach until Newman arrived on 4 June.

Newman's combative personal style is described by historian Karen Mason: "Newman relished the picketing and took great delight in her ability to elude the police sent to arrest her, as her face was not yet known to them. She preferred the picket line to the negotiating table."[16] In a statement to the *Kalamazoo Telegraph Press*, Newman was characteristically blunt: "I am supposed to play the part of the diplomat when I would rather be the fighter. It's more natural to fight than to be diplomatic. Being diplomatic makes you a hypocrite. You say yes when you mean no, and smile when you feel like frowning. But you do it because you think some good may come of it."[17]

Neither Casey and Barnum's "ladies" nor Newman's "fighters" won the day in Kalamazoo. By June the strike was winding down to an unsatisfactory conclusion. Strikers went back to work on June 15. Soon afterward they voted to renew the strike. But the different organizational and rhetorical strategies employed by Casey, Barnum, and Newman went deeper than style. They represented fundamentally distinct conceptions of gender and class. Casey's focus on moral issues emphasized women's vulnerability and reinforced traditional notions of gender difference. Newman's socialist orientation directed attention to women's economic role as consumers and urged "unladylike" behavior on the picket line.[18] Both sought victory, but the former argued from a position familiar to nineteenth-century social reformers: women were socially important precisely because they were more fragile than men. In contrast, Newman advised women to violate conventional norms for women and to adopt male behaviors. In brief, Casey and Barnum, through their conduct of the strike, emphasized the difference between men and women; Newman's approach underscored the similarity.[19]

But Newman learned harder lessons in the sexual politics of the labor movement during her years on the road, lessons that led her to modify her notions of what was possible for women through the labor movement. The rigid hierarchy that still characterizes the ILGWU—a male leadership and a large female rank and file—took shape during those years. Many male workers and union leaders regarded the woman worker as a threat to wage levels and believed her uncommitted to the union. "Chickens in a china shop," union leader Benjamin Stolberg called female activists.[20] Union bosses continued to send organizers like Newman out on the road rather than rewarding them with leadership positions in New York.[21]

While publicly counseling working women to stand shoulder to shoulder with their male comrades, Newman privately expressed her frustration with trade union and socialist men to her friend Rose Schneiderman. "If ever I had a spark of hope for our Jewish movement, I lost it now. . . . They have no manners and no sense. I do not feel at home with them anymore."[22] But Newman was equally disenchanted with the middle-class reformers she met in organizing campaigns. By and large she found the WTUL allies naive and ineffective in speaking to working women.

Newman believed that the "girls" were hard to organize largely because the workers had internalized conventional sex roles: they tried to behave with ladylike reserve rather than forthrightly, with pluck. In her speeches and writings Newman therefore emphasized the common interests of men and women and their shared problems as workers even as she acknowledged the practical issues involved in organizing women. She advocated separate organizations for women not because women were different or morally superior but for purely strategic reasons. In 1913 she wrote, "We all know that girls feel more at home among themselves than among men. Then again, when they meet together with men they hardly get a chance to express their opinions on questions that concern them."[24]

In her columns for the labor and feminist press she acknowledged that women posed a unique challenge for organizers and was not above appealing to "feminine" sensibilities and concerns.[25] At the same time, she recognized that women's roles in the twentieth century were different from those of their foremothers. When thousands of women marched in the Labor Day parade in 1911, she joyfully proclaimed, "'The world does move!' For not so very long ago it was very difficult to get the American working woman to parade, or to take part in any public demonstration; she considered it as a man's job, the man thought that it was not womanly to parade through the streets. . . . Times, however, have changed."[26]

Fundamentally, though, Newman was a social environmentalist, not an essentialist.[27] She believed that men and women were cut from the same human cloth, were shaped by historical circumstances, and were distinguished by different social and economic roles. She railed at middle-class reformers who argued for suffrage on the basis of women's superior moral capacities, for they would make of "women a near divinity and of man a mere side issue." As a socialist she feared that such distinctions created an unbridgeable gap between working-class and middle-class women.

She demonstrated her approach to the problem of class and gender by taking a prominent role in the New York suffrage campaigns of 1915 and 1917. As a member of the Socialist Suffrage Campaign Committee, she struggled to bring female emancipation to the center of socialist discourse. Her serious face, wire-rimmed glasses, and sensible hat appeared on large posters advertising her lectures. But she also campaigned for suffrage under the banner of the National American Women's Suffrage Association. Newman feared that her leftist associations would discredit her with the suffragists, who were looking for working women who could campaign to help them gain credibility among working men. When Rose Schneiderman introduced Newman to

NAWSA president Carrie Chapman Catt, Newman thought it well to warn Catt of her leftist affiliations. She recalled, "Having known before that Mrs. Catt and her colleagues were on the conservative side, I said, 'Mrs. Catt, I want you to know I'm a socialist.'" Catt's weary reply was: "Who isn't?"[28]

Despite Catt's sense of the ubiquity of the socialist suffragist, female suffrage posed a knotty problem for American socialists. Although women's suffrage was compatible with the socialist philosophy of equal rights, the notion of cross-class cooperation with mainstream suffragists threatened the class-conscious orientation of the Socialist Party of America. Newman understood that, ironically, the suffrage and socialist movements of the time shared more than each recognized. Both believed in social evolution, and both saw the political subordination of women as ineffective in modern society. What the socialists called "capitalism" the suffragists termed "industrialism," but each linked the phenomenon with a wide array of social problems.[29]

In Newman's numerous speeches and essays, with characteristic pragmatism, she termed suffrage "only a means to an end. A weapon to achieve our ultimate goal . . . to regulate and finally abolish the evils from which the working class suffers." At the same time, though, when writing for her socialist comrades, she stressed the social responsibility of motherhood and confidently asserted that women would use the ballot with "more wisdom" than men had done. In Newman's opinion, a national law to abolish child labor, for example, would naturally follow women's enfranchisement.[30]

While other socialists debated the "correctness" of participation in the mainstream suffrage movement, Newman demonstrated integrationist rather than separatist tendencies among socialists.[31] Newman's references to regulatory legislation and gender difference reflected the influence of reformist thinking, just as she represented the perspective of workers among reformers, particularly the WTUL. In Newman's writings, it is clear that while suffrage would empower the working woman, it would also unite workers of both genders by giving them as a class a voice in American politics. Even after suffrage had been won, she challenged readers of the labor paper the *Message* with an essay entitled "Are You Ready to Use Your New Power?" She celebrated the sweet victory but reminded her trade union readers that they had a duty to perform in their responsible exercise of the franchise, "a duty not only to themselves, but to their class."[32]

Suffrage formed a key component of Newman's feminism during these years of intense political ferment. To her, feminism clearly meant a commitment to suffrage and to improved industrial conditions for women and also a faith in the capacity of socialism to effect positive social change. In the years that she spent honing her political beliefs in the various organizations, and in the long talk fests over pie and coffee at Child's, she also struggled to achieve clarity in her personal life. Her remarkably frank correspondence with her beloved friend Rose Schneiderman shows that her mood fluctuated from elation to despondency. She was often restless and frequently lonely while on the road. She longed to have Rose share her pleasures and adventures and sometimes was "just crazy to have a long talk" with her absent friend.[33]

Any long talk certainly would have included a discussion of suitors and romance. A relationship with Frank Bohn, a socialist comrade, seems to have lasted about a year, although she admitted to being a "Puritan" in regard to sex. Following an interlude with him, she mourned, "For he is now going away on a long journey. I do not know where my next night lodging would be and so I like so many will live with memories that blur and burn of barren gain and bitter loss." Newman found other suitors while on her various speaking tours but discovered, at least in her twenties, that her need for an independent life outweighed her desire for security.[34]

Her independence seemed a prerequisite for her work as a writer or a journalist. In 1911, she confidently wrote to Rose, "The more I write, the more certain I feel I could succeed." The following year she dreamed of seeing her first book in print, but she reassured Rose, "Believe me that it is not the joy of seeing my name in the paper that I like about my writing, but rather the fact that my English is at last being accepted, and that I am getting hold of the technical points, such as the punctuations, grammar, etc, without having anybody to help me."[35]

Like Barnum and Dreier, Newman found fiction a powerful vehicle through which to express her thoughts and experiences. In 1912 she based a short story on an incident that occurred while she was on an organizing tour. The fictional "Mr. Hodge," a sixty-year-old farmer, writes to "Miss Vera," a Chicago factory worker, and asks her to marry him. She is sorely tempted, since she yearns for the joys of country life, but she believes that such a marriage would mean "selling myself for food and shelter." She remains "true to herself" and stays in the city.[36] Newman's "Vera" invites comparison with the fictional characters created by Barnum and Dreier, who faced similarly demanding questions about work and romance. Mr. Hodge is as inappropriate a suitor for Vera as Barbara Richards's first beau was for her. Newman, though, made a bolder narrative choice for her heroine than Barnum or Dreier—there is only independence to offer Vera satisfaction, no romantic marriage, and no leftist Mr. Right to tell her that her commitment to work makes her especially attractive.

Newman's desires recall Anzia Yezierska, the novelist, in her struggles between tradition and becoming modern. One historian, writing of Yezierska, could have been describing Newman as well when she observed that "at its extreme, when a woman's autonomy involved the search for personal fulfillment, it became nothing short of revolutionary. It violated a basic tenet of Jewish family structure: that women were merely the servants of men, the extensions of their husbands."[37] Like Yezierska, Newman turned her back on Judaism and its family traditions.[38]

Newman understood the limitations of conventional marriage and bridled against the restraints of conventional sex roles. Yet her desire for intimacy and companionship continually surfaced in her letters to Schneiderman. Newman did not resolve the conflict between her emotional needs and her fear of involvement for many years. But during her peripatetic years as an organizer she increasingly found solace more in the company of middle-class reformers than in Jewish immigrant culture, which barely tolerated independent and ambitious women.

The community of women that Newman found in the various clubhouses of the WTUL was a welcome relief from the quarrels and discrimination of the union. She still found the WTUL "allies" naive and ineffective in speaking to working women. About Margaret Dreier Robins, Newman wrote, "You know that I think an awful lot of Mrs. Robins but the only fault I find with her is that she has made all the girls of the League think her way and as a consequence they do not use their own mind, and do not act the way they feel, but the way Mrs. Robins wants them to." The teas and social events sponsored by the League were inspired by the "instinct of charity rather than unionism." Yet her WTUL friends accompanied her on treasured trips to operas and theater, and they provided vacation homes for the weary campaigner. She remembered the novelty of her first vacations; it was "quite an experience to do nothing but eat and sleep and read."[39]

Newman asked Schneiderman, "How long more will I be on the go? Will I never have a place where I could rest and do things I desire most?" She began to find an answer in 1913. She accepted a position as a factory inspector for the Joint Board of Sanitary Control and for the next four years worked primarily in New York City. These were years of peak suffrage activity as well, during which Newman continued her triple allegiance to the union, socialism, and the WTUL. Newman's reputation as an authority on women and industrial conditions brought her invitations to speak at college classes. The Russell Sage Foundation, impressed with Newman's article on maternity insurance, consulted her on the problem of how to insure working women against illness. In 1919, Newman traveled to Canada to address the Canadian Labor Congress as a representative of the American labor movement. She probably did not mention her weariness in her discussion of U.S. trade unions and the WTUL. Whatever her private misgivings, the self-assured labor leader preparing to speak before thousands of foreign unionists had clearly traveled a long way from the insecure young factory worker of a decade before.

Despite her recognition by her contemporaries, one would be hard pressed to place Newman in any of the familiar interpretive schemes about Progressive Era women. Historians have delineated women's role in the construction of the welfare state, have shown how they used tactics of moral suasion in women's strikes, and have traced the redefinition of womanhood to include the image not only of mother but also of wage earner.[40] Historian Alice Kessler-Harris, for example, identifies two types of activist women: those who chose to work within the labor movement and those who, like Rose Schneiderman, committed themselves to organizations parallel to "an organized labor movement they supported but did not fully trust."[41] Yet Newman's involvement with the feminist WTUL was as extensive as her work with the ILGWU; her strike strategy was expressed in "economic" rather than "moral" terms; and her endorsement of maternity insurance linked motherhood with wage earning.

Newman, and other activists, circumvented the limitations of both the trade union and the moral reformist approaches to social problems by demanding that the state take responsibility for the welfare of workers, families, and women. In 1916, she had made one of the first of many appearances before the New York state legislature. The issue at hand was a health insurance bill with a maternity clause proposed by the American Association for Labor Legislation. Newman, arguing for the bill, contended that the state was responsible for the well-being of children. The legislators, fearful then as now that wage work for women would undermine the family, asked whether maternity insurance would attract women to wage work. Of course not, Newman replied. "*It is the struggle for existence*, not maternity benefit that does and will drive married women into industry."[42]

The inevitable struggle for existence also led Newman and the WTUL to endorse maternity insurance as well as a range of industrial legislation in the 1920s. For its organizational efforts, the WTUL targeted women workers in textiles, laundries, hotels, and restaurants, where conditions were particularly debilitating. WTUL leaders reasoned that legislation regulating hours and wages would make workers more responsive to organizing efforts.

How did Newman come to support welfare state policies? Certainly the involvement of the state in social problems dovetailed with her socialist philosophy. Newman never stopped being a socialist, but once welfare state policies had embraced the goals of the eight-hour day, the five-day week, and the decent wage, little but the spiritual essence remained of the socialism Newman knew.[43]

Moreover, the WTUL endorsed legislation as its primary strategy for effecting change. Between 1918 and 1923, the League was Newman's institutional and political center. While she was "on loan" from the ILGWU to the Philadelphia WTUL, Newman became a familiar figure in the Pennsylvania state legislature lobbying for labor legislation. She played an important role in policy formation in the League. In 1919 she chaired the Committee on the Organization of Leagues. She urged the League to organize in the South and, in a pragmatic recognition of the changing realities of the labor marketplace, to develop strategies to organize black women.[44]

During her time in Philadelphia, Newman learned more about the difficulties of working within a male-dominated labor movement. In the 1920s, it became apparent that equal rights for women, while demanded by the labor movement's philosophy of moral justice, were more often than not an abstraction. Local unions frequently found women workers threatening and unstable.[45]

These attitudes caused Newman's repeated disillusionment with the labor movement. In the ILGWU, her own union, the General Executive Board quashed an attempt by Local 25, the largest and most militant of the women's locals, to gain "a greater voice in union affairs." In 1922, following a successful campaign to organize candy workers in Philadelphia, the international office refused to grant the fledgling union a charter. Even the solidarity that Newman had come to expect among union women of the "generation of 1909" dissolved in the 1920s. Newman spoke crisply of Clara Lemlich's communism: "Her politics was [*sic*] not my cup of tea. We no longer had anything in common except the memory of the strike and our participation in it."[46]

While a sense of woman as different had helped reformers highlight the plight of the woman worker in earlier decades, the perception of difference was now used by the labor movement to exclude women from certain trades and hours through protective legislation. The notion was that woman's inherent weakness in the workplace was better addressed by the state. As a trade union woman caught in the various contradictions of the historical moment, Newman found herself in a situation that historian Alice Kessler-Harris has described as "being part of, and yet not part of—this was the dilemma of the woman trade unionist of the 1920s."[47]

Newman resolved the professional and political dilemma by relying more on reformist methods like labor legislation. But she never fully left the socialist and trade union camps to embrace feminist reform. Thinking pragmatically, as always, she saw that the women workers most in need of protection fell outside the trade union net. Indeed, except in the garment industry, the male labor movement showed indifference, if not hostility, to the organization of women workers. Legislation, then, seemed the most expedient and effective way of improving the lot of the woman worker, of ending the working conditions that had produced the Triangle fire.

But during her years in Pennsylvania, Newman managed to resolve her personal quandary about independence and companionship. She wrote of her increasing awareness that "there is a world outside the trade union movement . . . a world of books and art, and the beauty of nature, a world which invited me to get to know it, to admire and to love it."[48] The longing for culture and education attracted Newman to a new and important friend in Philadelphia.

In 1918, Newman met Frieda Miller, the woman who would

become her life companion. Both women roomed at the College Club in Philadelphia. During the great flu epidemic that swept across much of the United States in 1917–1918, Newman nursed her new friend back to health from near death. Miller embodied much that Newman emulated. A member of an established Wisconsin family, she had studied economics at the University of Chicago, where, as Newman noted with admiration, "she studied fine arts and law as well." Newman remembered Miller as "a very vivacious, cheerful, knowledgeable, kindly person. She was a person who loved life. She was concerned with people, loved music . . . literature . . . the country . . . nature . . . loved all that is enjoyable and knowledgeable."[49] Shortly after her recovery, Miller left her position as instructor of economics at Bryn Mawr College to become secretary of the Philadelphia WTUL, joining Newman in labor reform.

Were they lovers? Certainly they loved each other and shared a long life together. These facts alone would lead many to define Miller and Newman as lesbians. For historian Blanche Cook, "women who love women, women who choose women to nurture and support and to create a loving environment in which to work creatively and independently, are lesbians."[50] But Newman and Miller would clearly have been uncomfortable with the label.[51] They belonged to a generation that felt it appropriate to leave certain aspects of personal life unarticulated. Elisabeth Burger, Frieda Miller's daughter, described their relationship in a way perhaps most pleasing to both of them: Newman was, quite simply, "my mother's best friend."[52]

In 1923, Frieda Miller left Philadelphia for the International Congress of Working Women in Vienna. Newman soon joined her, and after the meetings they traveled through Europe to England. Sometime during this trip Miller delivered a child.[53] When all three returned to the United States, they established a household in Greenwich Village. Newman took a new position with the ILGWU Health Center, and Miller held various positions in New York welfare organizations until she became director of the New York state division of Women in Industry in 1929.

Once, when asked about their unusual household, Elisabeth Burger replied that she never considered it unusual. The avant-garde world of 1920s Greenwich Village included other families like theirs. Of her classmates at the progressive City and Country School and later at Friends Seminary High School, few came from conventional nuclear families. Burger did remember, however, the positive effect of growing up in a world of idealistic women and "knowing that women worked, that women talked shop and cared about politics and that they ran their own lives. And I knew that when I was old enough, I would find a job that would enable me to try to make the world a better place."[54] The rich texture of Newman and Miller's lives as Burger remembered them attests to an important historical fact about their generation of women. Networks of love and support sustained large numbers of activist women in politics and the professions. During the early part of the twentieth century, women found that other women could accept the fullness of work and the politics of activism without expecting the compromises that more conventional domestic arrangements demanded.[55]

But when speaking of the social world centered on their apartment and their Connecticut summer home, Burger described more than a circle of friends. She painted a picture of a feminist culture, a world peopled by women who shared a history of political activity in suffrage and labor reform.

> Our apartment was a lively place where women like Rose Schneider-man, Elisabeth Christman and Mabel Leslie, all active in the Women's Trade Union League, were often joined by other New York women such as Elinore Herrick, Director of the New York Regional Office of the NLRB [National Labor Relations Board], Judge Dorothy Kenyon, and Bess Bloodworth, head of personnel at the old Namm department store in Brooklyn. They talked shop a lot, but it was a lively kind of discussion and there were jokes and fun and there was time out for good food. On New Year's Eve, there was always a poker game that began after dinner. The stakes were very low but it was a big event and they would dress up for it. Pauline would wear one of her hand embroidered dresses from the Peasant Art Shop.[56]

Weekends were spent at the vacation home in Connecticut, which was crowded with sister reformers eager to share each other's company and ideas.

The feminist culture in which Miller and Newman participated so fully gave them more than emotional support for their professional lives. Throughout the 1920s and especially in the 1930s, members of their network rose to influential positions in government and labor. Because of ties among them, a feminist agenda and a distinctly gendered language became a prominent part of New Deal reform and the creation of the welfare state.[57] The personalized nature of the feminist culture and its "strong sense of community . . . kept alive a somewhat autonomous women's political culture even after they [the reformers] entered mainstream politics."[58]

By 1923, Newman had come into her own. The "soul yearning" that she described so poignantly to Rose Schneiderman ten years earlier had been satisfied by a partner and a child. She was a recognized authority on the American working woman, and through the WTUL she had successfully combined her feminism with her commitment to the labor movement. Perhaps more than the other women I describe in this book, Newman faced a complicated task of self-definition and self-representation. Yet she, perhaps most fully of the four, negotiated the meaning of wage work for women and charted the distance between the pigheaded girl and the Triangle fire. Writing for labor and reform papers satisfied her youthful creative ambitions, her friendships with women reformers addressed her need for community, and her household with Frieda and Elisabeth fulfilled her desire for intimacy. While she well knew what her experience brought to the WTUL and how it enhanced her credibility at legislative hearings, she was also aware of the material comfort and intellectual stimulation provided by her personal life.

Newman's middle years were deceptively quiet by comparison with her earlier period of political and personal turmoil. The great uprisings, the whistle-stop tours, and the vibrant socialist culture of the teens had passed into history, to be replaced by a conservative, antilabor milieu in the 1920s.

The 1920s also saw a devastating civil war within the ILGWU. Faced with a Communist insurgency within its own ranks and with competition from nonunion shops, ILGWU membership plunged from 105,400 members in 1920 to 32,300 members by the end of the decade. The union entered the 1930s having won a Pyrrhic victory over the Communists.[59] The battle hit Newman particularly hard. Not only did she become alienated from many of her comrades of the generation of 1909, but as resources drained out of the ILGWU in the 1920s, the Health Center found itself in jeopardy. In 1929, Newman mounted a defense of the center. She obtained credentials from union president Morris Sigman so that she could approach other unions for support. "I spent my days and nights at their meetings and I did get the money and they sent their members who needed medical care to the health center."[60]

The Union Health Center, which continues to function today, is a clinic and referral service for union members. It was a corner of the union that embodied Newman's ideas about the union as a social welfare agency. In the 1990s it still offers health education outreach and social services. Newman's contributions to developing and administering the center's programs led union bureaucrats to depict her as a "patient advocate" who was the center's "soul." Newman agreed with the statement published in the *Industrial Bulletin*: "In all of her service to the Center, Miss Newman has used a simple human approach to the countless problems that have arisen. She is sure that scientific methods and procedures of administration are valuable but personally she is inclined to leave statistics to statisticians and other who enjoy them. To her the purpose of the Health Center is to help people."[61] Newman's "simple, human approach" cloaked her considerable talents and energies as a fund-raiser, patient advocate, and liaison between the polyglot patient population and the medical establishment.

Newman was also kept busy in the 1920s by open shop campaigns in Pennsylvania and New York. Through the WTUL she successfully organized Black and Hispanic laundry and hotel workers. She also took on increased responsibilities for the educational and administrative mission of the Health Center. She started programs that anticipated New Deal ideas about public responsibility for social welfare. Her vision of unionism set her apart from the "union bureaucrats" who headed the ILGWU and other large unions in the 1920s.

Newman's tripartite approach to the situation of the woman worker—organization, legislation, and education—was compatible with the industrial feminism of the WTUL.[62] Influenced perhaps by her increased involvement with the WTUL and the pragmatic realities of women's situation in the workplace and the union, Newman began to use concepts of difference rather than sameness to shape her arguments about the woman worker. By the 1920s, Newman's defiant description a decade earlier of women as men's equals more nearly approached the views being propounded by other feminists. She was as vociferous as Mary Dreier, if not more so, in her opposition to the ERA.

When she spoke on the ERA, Newman enjoyed particular credibility with working women. At a 1922 conference of trade union women sponsored by the Legislative Committee of the WTUL, for example, Newman unequivocally condemned the "blanket amendment." "We know what is equality and what is not. Experience has taught us that. There are so-called equal rights which furnish thrills for the few, but have no regard for the lives of the many. We want to remove discriminations, but a blanket law that threatens to take away rights already won we will fight, and fight to a finish."[63]

The support of protective legislation, with its implicit acknowledgment of women's difference, was, as we have seen, a hallmark of women's labor activism in the postsuffrage period. But it put women in an ambiguous position within the labor movement. Before the 1930s, women won labor battles less through economic channels and demand for bread-and-butter goals than "by relying on public support, indignation and protest." Their "moral outrage" and the "special claims" of motherhood publicly defined laboring women and thereby gave them a self-conscious women's culture. While this shared indignation effectively generated and maintained female union membership in the teens, it put women out of synch with the "oligarchic character" of the trade union movement in the 1920s. The garment workers, in particular, continued to have a large female rank and file governed by a small male leadership elite. Adrift in a hostile antilabor sea in the 1920s, male unionists saw women, particularly once their difference had been highlighted, as "weak and unreliable allies." The tension between male and female unionists played itself out in the struggle over the ERA, which continued into the 1970s. For women like Newman, the fight meant a "resuscitation of the spirit of community that prevailed in the prewar period," but "male trade union leaders . . . understood protective legislation as a way of restraining women's demands for admission into their organization, and opposed the amendment all too willingly."[64]

Newman's papers abound with invitations to debate the ERA question, with pamphlets that outline the liabilities of the proposed amendment, and with references to her membership in such groups as the Campaign Committee against the Equal Rights Amendment and the National Committee to Defeat the Unequal Rights Amendment. The ERA did more than threaten protective legislation statutes. It also brought labor reformers like Newman into direct conflict with professional women of the National Women's Party and highlighted the deep fissure in American feminism in the postsuffrage period. Newman "took on" these elite women and described her credentials as a spokesperson for the woman worker with pride:

> The leadership of that party is [in] the hands of those whose wealth permits them to commute from New York or Paris and preach the gospel of an unrestricted working day. I claim that not until Mr. Broun, Mrs. Belmont, and other "champions" of "equality" have worked ten and more hours a day in a laundry or foundry have they any right to opposed the forty-eight hour week for women workers.

Not until Mrs. Hooker, and Miss Hale (Mrs. Haywood Broun) have had to scrub floors at thirty cents an hour have they any right to oppose minimum wage legislation. Not until they have spent several years in a Southern textile mill have they any right to oppose special legislation for working women. Until they have done that they had better leave the question of industrial legislation to industrial women.[65]

Newman differed from like-minded feminists such as Mary Dreier in that her opposition to the ERA reflected her own experience as a worker as well as her familiarity with the needs and desires of other women workers. In her overlapping identities—union bureaucrat, WTUL leader, and authoritative spokesperson called before scores of state and federal legislative and investigative panels—these credentials mattered. She helped determine policy in a world where the state's role in shaping workers' lives was displacing that of the AFL with its voluntarist philosophy.

The defense of protective legislation by feminists such as Newman thus presents a troublesome paradox. Newman cannot be dismissed as out of touch with the thoughts or needs of the average worker. Protective legislation aimed, in a sense, to level the playing field between male and female workers. Such a position demanded that feminists support the limiting ideology of difference while at the same time putting them in the vanguard of reform. As Diane Kirby points out, feminists "sought to incorporate the state into the labor contract through legislation," a particularly prescient position that recognized that the "AFL's 'voluntarist' approach to industrial relations was ineffective in an era of corporate growth and technological innovation."[66] By the 1930s and 1940s, however, as unions expanded, and certainly by the 1970s, when a new generation of feminists recognized the limitations of protective legislation, women workers stood to gain more than they would lose from the ERA. Reformers like Newman and Dreier were blind to the advantages in part because they had so vilified the opposition. Newman undoubtedly agreed with one of her correspondents in 1938 who wished that the "Women's Party would move to Germany enmasse."[67]

The Women's Trade Union League formed the counterpoint to the Women's Party throughout the 1930s and 1940s. Its reformist politics rode into mainstream political life through Eleanor Roosevelt. Even when Franklin Roosevelt was governor of New York, the League had access to the highest level of state government. In 1929, 300 members celebrated the twenty-fifth anniversary of the WTUL in grand style at the Roosevelts' Hyde Park home. A chartered boat brought them up the Hudson for a festive program that reached its climax in an eight-act pageant written by Mary Dreier. In pantomime and song the cast commemorated the "triumphant" progress made in improving workshop conditions for women.[68]

It is tempting to speculate about Pauline Newman's frame of mind as she took part in this joyful singing and marching. Surely she had found in her mature years a community akin to the Socialist Literary Society of her youth. But had her disdain and distrust for middle-class reformers become a thing of the past? Did the elegant surroundings of Hyde Park and the Roosevelts awe her? Had she, like the labor leader Sidney Hillman, made the "long journey from Debsian socialism to New Deal liberalism"? Whatever her private feelings, her public support and admiration for FDR were clear.

Given her personal observation of Roosevelt's support for issues she cared deeply about, it should come as no surprise that Newman kept a portrait of FDR in her office and explained his popularity with the statement, "All the people who suffered from 1909 on could hope in this man and he fulfilled their hopes."[69]

Newman and her sister reformers were often guests at Hyde Park while Roosevelt was governor. When the women gathered with Eleanor, FDR sometimes joined them for discussions of politics and labor. These were more than social occasions. The labor law and policy that developed in New York state during the Smith-Roosevelt years became models for programs implemented at the federal level when Roosevelt became president. The WTUL women knew that their ideas were falling on receptive ears.

FDR brought labor with him into the White House in 1933. The founding of the CIO, the industrial warfare of the great sit-down strikes, and the possibilities opened by New Deal labor legislation infused new energy into the moribund labor movement and made the 1930s the decade of labor. Industrial unions like the ILGWU seized opportunities created by the National Recovery Administration (NRA) and the Wagner Act (National Labor Relations Act). Soon after the passage of this legislation, ILGWU organizers reported well-attended meetings of dues-paying members and a huge jump in union membership.

During the "turbulent years," Newman was in her midforties and part of a household with a young child. Her public role centered on New York. She was a member of state manpower commissions, advisory boards, children's boards, and Women's Bureau committees. Like Dreier, she joined the American Labor Party. She continued to be a sought-after witness on protective legislation before various legislative committees.[70]

In some ways, Newman's activities in the 1930s transcended the New Deal. Many unorganized and poorly paid women such as laundry and domestic workers fell between the cracks of New Deal protections. Newman, appointed to negotiate a state minimum wage for laundry workers, was able to get New York laundry workers an hourly wage that surpassed the federal standard. Newman also worked along with other WTUL lobbyists on behalf of domestic workers to obtain more equitable minimum-wage standards on a state level than would be possible through federal legislation. All in all, between 1937 and 1942, Newman was appointed by the state to investigate wage scales and negotiate minimum wages for women in five different industries.

Her increased involvement in government committees and commissions has tempted some to see Newman as a failed leftist and her youthful socialism as coopted by the New Deal's liberalism. By the 1930s, it had become increasingly difficult to label Newman's politics. While she still considered herself a socialist, there are both indications of her conservatism and ways in which she had cast her lot with liberals.[71] In her mind, though, the principal goal that she had worked for in her youth—security for workers—had been accomplished by the New Deal. As far as she was concerned, the fact that the agent of change was a Democratic administration rather than socialist was immaterial. What mattered was that workers enjoyed the security of unemployment insurance, labor standards, and a minimum wage and that these reforms not only made shops cleaner and safer but also improved homes and family life. Mindful of labor's debt after almost twenty years of a Democratic White House, she expressed fears of what an Eisenhower administration would mean for labor and progressive causes.[72]

Almost twenty years after the beginnings of the New Deal, in a Labor Day essay written for the *Jewish Daily Forward*, Newman defined "Labor's Unfinished Business." She applauded the phenomenal progress made by labor in her lifetime, then expressed hope that the future would bring a united labor movement, equal pay for equal work, and "responsible positions" for women in the labor movement. Despite the gains of the past two decades, women workers were still largely unorganized; to meet their needs, Newman continued to promote the dual strategy of legislation and organization. She sounded the call, "Let Labor Day of 1952 be a day of decision—to organize, to educate, and to advance the position of women in our beloved country."[73]

In 1952, this elder stateswoman of labor wrote from a perspective different from that of the uncompromising young radical forty years earlier. Newman had appeared before numerous legislative committees in Albany and Washington, had investigated conditions of labor for women in postwar Germany, and was a U.S. delegate to International Labor Organization (ILO) commissions on domestic servants in 1951 and 1952.

Her overlapping roles in labor, feminism, and government had given Newman and others like her a social vision that was ahead of the times in acknowledging the double role of modern women in the household and the shop. These women recognized the limitations of education, legislation, and organization in alleviating the problems of the woman worker, but they knew that her best hope lay in a combination of all three approaches. They sought to transcend trade boundaries through such organizations as the WTUL and national boundaries first through international conferences of working women and later through League of Nations and United Nations organizations like the ILO.[74]

In the early 1950s, Pauline Newman began to reflect in a systematic fashion on her life's work and accomplishment. Her "personal myth"—a "set of less-than-conscious motivations which lie behind manifest attitudes and behavior, and which are organized into a decipherable pattern based on crucial developmental experiences"—first began to emerge in a long autobiographical letter that she wrote to Frieda Miller's grandsons, Hugh and Michael Owen.[75]

Newman set out her "personal myth" in the stories she told and retold to Hugh and Michael and in three extensive oral history interviews. These tales speak of an intrepid and determined young woman who made her way in the New World, found communities of like-minded people, and pursued social justice all her life. The "myth" includes little material about her private life and personal relationships, but it is colored by Newman's strong opinions on politics and personalities.

Newman's "metaphor of self" offers something beyond a sense of self. Her narrative strikingly resembles that of other Eastern European immigrants and supports the notion that the shared political and cultural values of groups emerge in the comparative analysis of personal narratives. In other personal narratives, Jewish subjects "generally portrayed themselves as active, autonomous agents, having functioned within a social tapestry heavily embroidered not only with personal but also with power relationships. . . . Jews spoke of having educated themselves, having struggled to get ahead—their language describ[ed] co-workers and shop in metaphors of family and home." Like Newman, other Jewish women were observed to be reluctant to discuss their personal lives.

Arguably, then, recent Jewish history and culture had given Newman and others like her a social template that they brought to their experiences in the New World, where they reinforced each other. As one scholar expressed it, "Political movements among East European Jews . . . were congruent with modern notions of history because they assumed the possibility that human action could bring about change in this world."[76]

In her later years, Newman thus offered her audience another paradox. In its substance her narrative asks us to see a woman who traveled a long distance from her origins, yet its shape reflects the strong cultural pattern of Eastern European Jews.

Although she did not explicitly comment on the subject, Newman seemed attracted to at least the cultural aspects of Judaism in later life. In 1964 and again in 1967 she visited Israel, where she made the customary trade unionist's pilgrimage to labor centers, the Dubinsky Hospital and other clinics. She wrote of her many contacts with the Histadrut (the Israeli labor movement). After returning from her first trip, she spoke about the work of Histadrut in Israel to the Workingmen's Circle Histadrut Organization at Histadrut House in New York. In the same year she spoke about Eleanor Roosevelt to the New York chapter of the Women's Division of Jewish Labor Organizations. Elisabeth Burger noted Newman's renewed ethnic orientation and commented that "the difference in background and class" between Newman and her mother "caused strains that grew rather than diminished over time."[77]

Early in the 1960s, Frieda Miller had an affair with a man whom she had met in India. The episode caused a painful break in her relationship with Newman. Newman bitterly confided to her daybooks, "There is nothing as dead as a broken friendship." She longed to share a sunset "with one who at one time was there to do just that—those days are gone never to return." After decades of sharing a household, Newman took her own apartment.

In 1967, the disillusionment and hurt began to fade. Miller's health began to fail rapidly. The two women had reconciled, and Newman's daybooks chronicle Miller's difficult journeys in and out of hospitals and nursing homes. On Thanksgiving Day,

1970, she sketched a verbal picture of her friend seated in a chair looking out a window in the nursing home. "What did she see?" Newman wondered. "What was she thinking? Coffeetown? of her travels?" And later, "My heart aches for her and for all of us."[78]

Miller died in 1972. Newman outlived her companion by eleven years. She never retired but went faithfully every day to her Health Center office, where she was a beloved figure to some, a nuisance to others, and to all a living symbol of the ILGWU's history. By the 1970s, few remained of her WTUL cohort. Her domestic life centered on Elisabeth and Elisabeth's children. Finally ill health forced her to leave her apartment and live with her beloved "Liz" in 1981. She died in 1986.

Newman's activist life was neither that of a genteel philanthropist like Mary Dreier nor that of a charismatic leader like Rose Pesotta, the subject of my next chapter. A Jewish social tradition shaped her politics and her activism, but American society allowed her a personal life that would have been unheard of in the shtetl. Like the other women whom I have studied, Newman was a pragmatist, not an ideologue. Her commitment was to social justice and an improved way of life for women workers. She was willing to try a variety of methods to reach her goals. Her criticism of inequity and injustice was unsparing and unremitting. Like Mary Dreier, she lived long enough to witness a new wave of reform in the 1960s and to comment on the tragedy of Vietnam. When young scholars arrived, eager to eulogize her, she met them sometimes with humor yet more often with impatience.

Scholars may debate the sources and meaning of Newman's contributions. Newman, however, never hesitated in her evaluation of her own life. She said, idealistically and unequivocally: "If I had to live my life all over again I'd do the same thing. . . . It was a satisfaction, it was a hope, it was a goal, it was a vision, it was a dream."

4

Rose Pesotta

1896–1965
"the world is my country"

Rose Pesotta wanted history to remember her. She published two memoirs, and her extensive papers not only chronicle an activist life but also reveal the most intimate details of her personal relationships. Even without this evidence, though, her place in history would be assured by her role as one of the first female vice presidents of a major labor organization. Her life merits attention because she was the leading female trade unionist of her day. Pesotta's career opens the world of labor and the Left to us during dramatic years of mass strikes, Communist purges, and international organizing. But her passion, intelligence, and complicated personality beckon the biographer as much as her public accomplishments.

Pesotta shared with the other women in my book a quixotic desire for social justice. Yet unlike the other three reformers, she lived outside frameworks of female networks and feminist organizations. She was never part of the women's culture that centered

on settlements, suffrage, or the Women's Trade Union League. She did not help "engender" the welfare state, for as an anarchist she resisted state solutions to social problems. She confronted the hardships of working women as forcefully as her contemporaries, however, and found different, if not always satisfactory, solutions. Yet we may ask the same feminist questions about Pesotta that we asked about the other activists. How did she reconcile her private and public lives? How did she propose to eliminate discrimination against women in the union and in the workplace? Who were her friends, who were her role models, and where was her community? How did gender affect her working life and her activism? How did she define womanhood, work, and class?

Like Barnum, Dreier, and Newman, Pesotta constructed herself through narrative but in a fuller, more elaborate, and more public way, through her two published memoirs. Taken together, these publications tell us that Rose Pesotta was born in 1896, the second of eight children, into a middle-class family in Derazhnya, a railroad town in the Russian Ukraine. Itsaak Peisoty, her father, was a grain merchant, and Masya, her mother, was active in the family business.[1] Pesotta, like Newman, attributed her concern for social justice to her "dynamic and unconventional" father, a politically outspoken man who "had the courage of his convictions, a deep sense of responsibility toward his fellow man, and was always ready to undertake any task for the good of the community." In line with his progressive yet practical political views, Itsaak Peisoty organized a cooperative in Derazhnya.[2] Years later Pesotta expressed regret that "a man of his intellectual capacity was fated to be wasted in a Tsarist Ghetto town in the Ukraine."[3] Understanding her father's displeasure that his first four children were girls, Pesotta and her sisters struggled to prove that they weren't "sissies," a struggle that endowed her, she claimed, with "pep, vim, and vitality."[4]

Pesotta, again like Newman, wrote less about her mother. Like many other Jewish women in the Russian Pale, Masya Peisoty went out to work every day, keeping the books and tending the shop of the family business. Pesotta seems to have been unaware that the tradition of work outside the home may have contributed to her later activities.[5] She did link her ambivalence about marriage and domesticity to her mother's example, however. As she wrote in 1934, "My mother, like millions like her—toiled a lifetime raising a large family. How many sleepless nights and agonizing days has she spent at their bedside watching over them and now? Gone to the four corners of the world—and she is left alone—the price of raising a family."[6]

In Pesotta's coming-of-age memoir, *Days of Our Lives*, Derazhnya appears as vivid as a Chagall painting of villagers and a boisterous family. The pungent aromas of Sabbath cooking and a year marked by the Jewish rituals of Rosh Hashanah, Yom Kippur, Succoth, Purim, and Hanukkah fill the book, while pogroms and the anti-Semitic Black Hundreds cast a dark shadow over her childhood memories.

Pesotta learned the Russian and Hebrew alphabets at home and later attended Rosalia Davidovna's school for girls, with its Russian curriculum and its clandestine classes in Jewish history and Hebrew. After two years at the school, she was needed at home to help care for her siblings, and home tutoring replaced formal schooling.

As important as her formal education, though, was her political apprenticeship in one of the many leftist groups in the Russian Pale. When her older sister Esther became involved in the local anarchist underground, Pesotta soon followed. Reading Kropotkin, Bakunin, and Proudhon and joining the political activity of young radicals, she glimpsed the possibilities of a wider world. She found role models in the movement, women who had bypassed traditional marriages to devote themselves to a revolutionary cause. The teenaged girl "visualized [herself] as one of them, giving up everything to aid in creating a new society based on freedom of thought and expression, with universal education work for all without coersion of the nagayka—the lash—and nurseries, kindergardens, playgrounds for children, and homes for the aged."[7]

Her idealistic dreams came up short when she discovered her

parent's plan to marry her to a village boy. She rebelled and longed to join her sister in America, where "a decent middle class girl can work without disgrace."[8] In 1913, "after months of argument and cajolery," her parents gave Pesotta permission to go to the New World.

Pesotta made her journey to America in greater style and comfort than most immigrants. Accompanied by her grandmother, she traveled second class, enjoying shipboard festivities and companions. But like Pauline Newman and thousands of other Russian Jewish girls, Pesotta found the road between the New York docks and the garment shops a short one. She was soon working in various shirtwaist factories while struggling to learn English. She joined ILGWU Local 25 and discovered that the Uprising of the 20,000 and the Triangle fire had become union legends, experiences that set the "generation of '09" apart from younger women in the shops.[9] In 1915 she helped the local to form the first education department in the ILGWU, and in 1920 her "excess energies" got her reelected to Local 25's executive board.

Like Newman, Pesotta found another world beyond the shops and the union. Having been radicalized in the Old World, she sought out like-minded anarchists in the New. Unlike Newman, though, Pesotta is silent about her leftist activities in her autobiographies and with good reason. Anarchism never wore the public face nor had the "respectable" membership of American socialism. Composed of numerous sectarian groups, it existed on the margins of American political life. Most Americans associated anarchists with Haymarket bombers and "Red" Emma Goldman. In a graphic demonstration of American intolerance for such radicals, six short years after her arrival in America, Pesotta watched the ill-fated ship *Buford* set sail for Russia with 246 deported radicals, including Emma Goldman and Pesotta's fiancé, Theodore Kushnarev.

Whereas Newman had gravitated toward socialism, Pesotta found community and support for her libertarian beliefs in the alternative culture that American anarchists attempted to create through the Modern School movement and a calendar of commemorative dates and rituals such as the anniversary of the Paris Commune. She found friends and sometimes lovers in the alternative culture that centered on picnics and summer camps and the plays and lectures often held at New York's International Anarchist Center.[10]

While for Newman socialism was a secular path away from the traditional Judaism of her family, anarchism for Pesotta was inextricably enmeshed with the radical political tradition of Eastern European Jewish culture. Because Pesotta had left Eastern Europe as an adolescent rather than as a child, had come of age in a more cosmopolitan environment, and had already become politically involved, she framed her political self differently. Newman parted from her family on the issue of her socialist activity, while Pesotta's adolescent struggle concerned an arranged marriage. Pesotta arguably immigrated to embrace the romantic possibilities of the New World. We must consider life stage, in other words, when we seek to understand how these women incorporated the political context around them into their developing sense of self.

Anarchism was Pesotta's ethical center and continued to be so throughout her life.[11] Long after the movement had ceased to have a coherent organizational structure in the United States, Pesotta evoked its precepts in her personal life. She was drawn to "the philosophy of the deed" by its celebration of the inherent goodness of the individual and its rejection of private property, the state, and authority. For Pesotta, anarchism was "a philosophy, placing HUMAN RIGHTS above property rights, wherein no government or church shall interfer [sic] with the fulfilment of material and spiritual freedom."[12]

Her almost mystical devotion to anarchist ideals was inspired by the premier anarchist of her day, Emma Goldman. Pesotta first heard Goldman speak in 1914, met her on Ellis Island in 1919 as she and Pesotta's fiancé were about to be deported, and corresponded extensively with her while Goldman was in exile. The friendship between the two women deepened during Pesotta's trip to Europe in 1937. Pesotta played a prominent role in mobilizing support for Goldman's return to the United States.[13] Pesotta's sister Esther made the telling statement, "Emma helped Rose to believe in anarchism like a rabbi believes in God."[14]

Like Goldman and other women attracted to the movement, Pesotta found support for a sexually free lifestyle in anarchist tenets of personal freedom.[15] Responding to an anonymous critic in 1934, she wrote: "The principle which I hold dearer than anything else in the world is FREEDOM, which I interpret thus: *my freedom ends where your freedom begins, this is the cardinal principle of anarchism.* If the man I love does not care for my love any more, I personally would never try to chain him to myself, nor would I hold the person whom he might love responsible for his chance of effection [*sic*]."[16]

During the 1920s, Pesotta was secretary for the *Road to Freedom*, an anarchist paper edited by Hippolyte Havel; it was the "first important English anarchist journal in the United States since the suppression of *Mother Earth* in 1917."[17] Pesotta rarely wrote for the periodical, but perusing its pages gives one a sense of the concerns of her close friends and associates.[18] Readers of the *Road to Freedom* would find dispatches from Emma Goldman exiled in Europe, eulogistic pieces on Ferrer and Kropotkin, and an occasional article on the sexual liberation of women.[19] By and large, a reader of the *Road to Freedom* during the 1920s and 1930s would find little difference between the concerns of anarchists and those of socialists and liberals: the Bolshevik dictatorship, the rise of fascism, and the Spanish Civil War. Even the Sacco and Vanzetti case, the issue that dominated the pages of the *Road to Freedom* in the 1920s, was a cause embraced by most American leftists and liberals. Sacco and Vanzetti, however, and later the Spanish Civil War, sharpened and defined Pesotta's political views.

In the eyes of their supporters, Sacco and Vanzetti were jailed because they were committed to anarchism, not because they were murderers. As a sister anarchist, Pesotta championed their cause during the seven years between their conviction and their execution. She frequented Boston as a member of the Sacco and

Vanzetti Defense Committee, searched endlessly for new evidence that would exonerate them, and maintained an extensive correspondence with Vanzetti. As the execution date approached in 1927, defense activity became more and more fevered. During the summer of 1927, Pesotta served as liaison between the defense committee and the labor movement, especially foreign language groups. Like a whirling dervish, she organized mass meetings in New York and was a featured speaker at rallies in Pennsylvania and Connecticut. When all efforts to free the pair failed, she went to Boston and stood vigil sadly on their execution day, 23 August 1927. She and Alfred Baker Lewis led thousands of sympathizers in a funeral procession. That day marked the start of a self-imposed exile from Boston that would last five years.[20]

Years later, Pesotta bitterly labeled Sacco and Vanzetti's execution "blood on the conscience of America." Although Paul Avrich and other historians suspect that Sacco and Vanzetti may have been partly guilty, Pesotta passionately believed in their innocence. Her quintessentially romantic nature led her to recall Sacco's statement when they first met—"When thousands kill one, that means the one has conquered"—and to treasure her letters from Vanzetti.[21]

Pesotta's years with the Sacco and Vanzetti Defense Committee coincided with her increased involvement with the International Ladies' Garment Workers' Union, activity that she, like many syndicalists, saw as a natural outgrowth of her anarchist principles. Criticized by more "simon pure" comrades, she bristled, "I still hold that anarchism is a human philosophy; we must have intercourse with human beings, we must actively participate in all social events. We must be among the people and teach them our ideal in practice, instead of fostering hatred and mistrust we must be ready at any time to work and teach the workers to use their own iniciative instead of following in blind obidience, if we consider the labor movements as a means to an end—we shall work within this labor movement to attain our goal." She criticized orthodoxy among anarchists, which made them no better than "jesuits and communists" in their ostracizing of "heretics," and rallied her comrades to leave their "cozy corners at their favorate cafeterias and their own club rooms and go into the places where life is lived in the raw."[22] To another comrade's harsh words, she replied that union organizing was "MY WAY of work for a new society."[23]

But she admitted to more personal associations with her work.

> When I was a child mother never trusted me anything to carry. As soon as I would get something into my hands she would always cry out: "you'll drop it, put it away you'll drop it" and no sooner would she say that down the thing went and always broke. But I grew up nevertheless and am able now to carry heavy, very heavy things and do not break them either. When Mother came to me and I told her and now I am able to carry anything without dropping it and I have an idea that the samething will happen to me now. I shall carry my burden of a paid official as best as I could; and contrary to the preconceived opinions of my comrades who are very eager to see me succumb I shall live to be able to tell my story.[24]

Did Pesotta feel that she needed to prove her competence to her mother? Had the movement become like a parent to her? Had this most antiauthoritarian of organizations—ironically—become a source of authority for her? Whatever her motives, it is clear that Pesotta saw herself, and wrote, as a "propagandist" in the front lines of social revolution. Anarchy, in her mind, might ride to victory in the United States through the vehicle of the labor movement.

The first test of the strategy came in the 1920s as communists threatened to gain control of the ILGWU. Making common cause with socialists like Newman, Pesotta and other ILGWU anarchists were on the front lines of the fight. The anarchist's usual antipathy toward communists was fueled in Pesotta when Bolsheviks murdered her father in 1920. The ILGWU was essentially refounded in its chronic struggles with Communists in the 1920s, and grateful union officials recognized Pesotta's contributions by appointing her an organizer in the late 1920s.[25]

Pesotta brought to organizing a charismatic personality, boundless energy, and a unique ability to empathize with the downtrodden. She also brought a substantial background in worker education. She had spent the summer of 1922 at the Bryn Mawr Summer School for Workers.[26] The social feminist program at the elite women's college developed an innovative curriculum and pedagogy designed for students with minimal basic education and aimed at tapping their work and life experience. Students like Pesotta who came in the program's early years encountered an "ambitious liberal arts program."[27] In a bucolic setting (classes were "held under shady green trees on beautifully kept lawns"), she joined over a hundred young women workers from all parts of the United States who had gathered to study "labor economics, political and social history, the relationship of women to the labor movement, English literature, appreciation of music." She recalled a progressive faculty and "tutors, daughters of wealthy families, young women amazingly tall, who never had to bend over a sewing machine in their growing years."[28] Whereas Newman's contact with reformers in Philadelphia had reshaped the direction of her life and had drawn her closer to liberal reformers, Pesotta found that the Bryn Mawr experience reinforced her anarchist ideals and whetted her appetite for further education.[29]

In 1924, she won a scholarship to Brookwood Labor College and spent the next two years on its campus in Westchester County, forty miles north of New York City. The labor journalist Len De Caux described the labor college on the Hudson in rhapsodic terms: "Labor idealists liked Brookwood. To the romantic, it had aspects of a quasi-Utopian colony. To the more practical, if optimistic, it was a step toward advancing labor from the rear end to the vanguard of progress. . . . Spiritually, Brookwood was a labor movement in microcosm—without bureaucrats or racketeers—with emphasis on youth, aspiration, ideals. . . . it was altogether enchanting."[30]

Brookwood was the best known of about forty workers' colleges active in the 1920s and 1930s. Founded in 1921 by the pacifists William and Helen Fincke and administered by Social Gospel reformer A. J. Muste, Brookwood was run as a cooperative. Students had a share in everything from faculty hiring and educational policy to custodial work. Brookwood resisted the American impulse to "educate workers out of their class." Its basic philosophy was anticapitalist and, to the consternation of the labor movement, often antiunion. By the late 1920s, Brookwood was under fire from the American Federation of Labor for its radicalism and from the communist *Daily Worker* as "class-collaborationist." But prominent liberals like John Dewey continued to champion the labor college and to celebrate its maverick stance. Some of the most prominent activists of the 1930s emerged from the ferment at Brookwood. The college's influence on the labor movement was so great during the period that historian Steven Fraser has called it a "cadre school for the CIO."[31]

Pesotta flourished at Brookwood. She acted with the Brookwood Players, took road trips with friends, and expressed hopes that education would become an integral part of the anarchist movement so that more young comrades could share the opportunities that she was enjoying. Years later when she encountered Brookwood friends on labor's battlefields in Flint and Akron,[32] it was as though she had realized the goal she had stated at Brookwood: to become "a handle to the tools."[33]

By 1933, Pesotta had begun to incorporate what she had learned through classes and fieldwork into her union organizing.[34] That year established her reputation as an unusually talented organizer. After a brief stint working in Los Angeles, where she was blackballed for union activity, Pesotta hitchhiked back to New York and demanded that ILGWU president David Dubinsky return her to Los Angeles to organize the largely Mexican labor force in the garment shops. In September 1933, she spearheaded a dressmakers' general strike in the face of antipicketing injunctions, hired thugs, and communist dual unions. She brilliantly kept both workers and the public engaged in the strike through Spanish-language radio broadcasts and ads in ethnic newspapers.[35] She organized a strike commissary to serve breakfast and lunch to strikers and often sent food home with picketers. She stimulated public sympathy for the strike by marching hundreds of strikers' children in Halloween costumes into the picket area. Despite her efforts, though, on 4 November, an arbitration board ruled against the strike and ordered workers to accept NRA minimum wages. Disappointed at first, Pesotta soon realized that the NRA had left the door open to union organizing and concluded that "our union is on the march in California."[36]

Buoyed by this spirit, she headed north to San Francisco. There she found even her organizing skills unequal to the task of penetrating Chinatown's sweatshops. She was frustrated that she had been able to find "the right tactics" to organize Mexicans in Los Angeles but not Chinese workers in San Francisco. Undeterred by her failure, she set about learning about Chinese-American history and culture so that she could better understand workers' resistance to the union message.[37]

Pesotta made a dramatic entrance into the ILGWU annual convention in Chicago in May 1934. Woman delegates, eager to have a woman in the union's leadership ranks, nominated her for a vice presidency on the General Executive Board. Pesotta, equally eager to return to the shops, accepted the nomination with great reluctance. She pessimistically contended that "the voice of a solitary woman on the General Executive Board would be a voice lost in the wilderness." To a large measure, she was correct in her conclusion that sexism was entrenched. But the personal loss of her "independence" disturbed Pesotta as much as the futility of her mission. In remembering "one of the most unhappy days of my life," she wrote, "I felt hot and cold at the same time. It seemed as if I were being dragged down by some dread force—like a swimmer caught in an undertow. I wanted to cry out in protest, but my throat felt paralyzed."[38]

Although Pesotta never lost the sense of discomfort with her position, even after becoming one of the most successful organizers in the United States, she did find satisfaction in her work. During the next ten years she carried the union message to workers in Puerto Rico, Detroit, Montreal, Cleveland, Buffalo, Boston, Salt Lake City, and Los Angeles. She joined the great labor upheavals of the 1930s in Akron, Ohio, and Flint, Michigan.

Sometimes her organizing activities were tales of triumph; at other times she met with defeat. Throughout, though, she believed, "To us no strike was lost. Whatever the immediate outcome, we eventually win."[39]

Pesotta regarded the union as a social organization. In 1934, she traversed Puerto Rico, holding open air organizing meetings in rural areas, where the poverty and starvation moved her to start classes for women in birth control, personal hygiene, and child care. Her activities in Puerto Rico probably demonstrated most clearly her belief that the union should provide for a wide range of worker's needs—the medical, the recreational, and the educational. Her vision fit the "new unionism," the socialist-inspired notion that workers should be organized by industry rather than by craft and that "a new social order . . . would empower workers and provide for their welfare on and off the shop floor."[40] As an anarchist, Pesotta believed that if workers' needs were met by a class-identified organization like a union, there would be no need to resort to the state. As an effective organizer, she knew that songs, picnics, food, and classes helped create a union culture that encouraged workers' loyalty to the union.[41] And she consistently acknowledged her distinctive role as a woman to "make the proper approach to the dressmakers," to "particularly . . . persuade the women" when "a woman's approach" was needed.[42]

What was the woman's approach? For Barnum, Dreier, and Newman, it was the feminism found in separate women's reform organizations like the Women's Trade Union League. Pesotta, though, acknowledged and reinforced the importance of traditional sex roles in the largely immigrant groups she sought to organize. As she wrote of her experience in Akron: "To the women I made a special appeal that they stand by their men."[43] Pesotta knew the relationship of family to labor militancy as she mobilized the wives of sit-down strikers in Akron and Flint. She knew that workers could be organized effectively only if one had knowledge of and sympathy for their lives outside as well as inside the shop.

But like contemporary feminists, she also mentored and encouraged young women. She mothered two Puerto Rican girls and brought them to the United States on Brookwood Labor College scholarships. She trained young women in Seattle to make "smooth short speeches" to women's clubs and to church and labor groups and was gratified when "overnight these former subservient workers had changed radically. They had found themselves, had gained a new faith. They felt at last that they 'belonged.' "[44] "No longer meek, they had learned to speak out against injustice and stand up for their rights."[45]

Part of Pesotta's "woman's approach" was to make the union a "home" for workers when she arrived in a city. She "brightened up" union headquarters to make it "warm and cozy." Then came the food. Pesotta believed that as an army marched on its stomach, so did a strike.[46] In Seattle there were hot waffle sandwiches with Norwegian cheese, in Montreal shrimp cocktail and chocolate cake, and in Boston corned beef, pumpernickel bread, and "ample firewater to wash down the edibles."[47] Pesotta tailor-made radio messages for specific audiences—in Akron, the comedy sketch "Fanny Fink," a takeoff on Fanny Brice's popular Baby Snooks show with a union theme; in Buffalo, the continuing "Adventures of Stella and Helen"; and in Catholic Montreal, French broadcasts featuring the words of Pope Leo XIII in support of unions. Like a proud parent at a family picnic, Pesotta always had a movie camera handy at union gatherings to film the "merry scene."[48] As her friend and lover Powers Hapgood once told her, she was "one of the few 'labor executives' . . . who participate in what the rank and file is supposed to do. . . . You can't ask the rank and file to do things you won't do yourself."[49]

While Pesotta was acutely aware of discrimination and sexism within the labor movement, gender was not the principal lens through which she viewed the world. She exhibited what some historians have called a "female consciousness." Pesotta's activism, like that of French bread rioters, Kansas miners' wives, and other Jewish activists, sprang "not from an idealized gender-specific sense of sisterhood but rather from an evolving notion of partnership and coparticipation with men along class and community lines."[50] In other words, although she was well aware of the specific problems of women at home and in the workplace, she felt that the class struggle took precedence.

Pesotta's "women's community" was her sister workers in the garment shops rather than the ladies of the Women's Trade Union League. Her sentimental view of the garment shop as a community of women is expressed in several short stories she wrote featuring ethnically diverse workers engaged in some woman-centered activity. The story "In the Shop" celebrates the wedding of a coworker, "Peggy." In a highly idealized setting, the older women share stories of their children and memories of their own honeymoons at Niagara Falls. In Pesotta's fictional formulation, as in her own life, work was a permanent part of the female life cycle. "Almost invariably after a brief fling at home life they return to the shop where they feel at home, young and alive. There is a warm stimulating spirit here without which life seems dull and lonely."[51] Her stories are permeated with a sense of female, not feminist, consciousness. In them, the shared experience of work and union membership transcends ethnic differences among women, and owners are a benign paternal presence.

Pesotta's fictional shop was not far removed from her own nostalgic fantasies while "on the road." In 1934, she remembered the companionship of the shop and wrote, "Gee! how I am tired of all this! and how I would welcome the light warm dress shop—the one I left in New York! Nothing like the freedom of a plain rank and file member of the union."[52] As in the realization of her fictional fantasies, when *Bread upon the Waters* was published in 1944, her sister workers at the Will Steinman factory clustered around her at a workplace autograph party, where dill pickles, corned beef and tongue sandwiches, lily cups of whiskey and club soda marked the event.

In 1942, the unrelenting sexism of the union leadership led Pesotta to resign from her organizing role and retreat into the dress shop. Pesotta's frustration with the union reached a boiling point during a two-year campaign in Los Angeles. In January, she returned to Los Angeles to find the union she had organized in 1933 in disarray. Sportswear had displaced dress manufacturing, Black and White Dust-Bowlers had replaced Latina workers, Communists were still a troublesome presence, and "there was mismanagement in the union . . . discord and petty jealousy among the officers, peanut politics."[53] Displaying characteristic imagination and energy, Pesotta picketed the garment industry's annual style show with twelve workers in evening dress. The image of workers coopting the costume of the elite is a compelling one. "Some were in dazzling white with black velvet coats, others wore different colored gown and furs. Several, from their appearance, might have been Park Avenue debutantes."[54] The demonstration inspired precisely the headlines Pesotta wanted but won her little support from "cynical oldsters" among the union leadership, whose "chief passion," as she disparagingly wrote, was "pinochle playing."[55]

Ignoring the criticism, Pesotta "set out to clean house with a vengance [sic]." She replaced communists with other union members and in five months worked through a backlog of cases for the National Labor Relations Board. In May she flew to New York to accept a third term as union vice president. Back in Los Angeles, she threw her energies into organizing—union-sponsored holidays to Santa Catalina Island with "song sheets and a leader with a good voice," historical and children's floats in the Labor Day parade, and parties with sympathetic movie stars.

The Japanese attack on Pearl Harbor on 7 December 1941, precipitated Pesotta's decision to return to the rank and file. Reflecting on the satifactions of what was to be her last organizing campaign, she wrote in *Bread upon the Waters*: "Working here in the last two years, despite all the obstacles set in my path, I had felt that what I was doing had importance. The long neglected and scattered dressmakers' local had been made whole again and was thriving, and the sportswear and cotton dress groups were solidly organized. More than 2,000 women workers had joined our ranks in this city in those two years and could be counted as good unionists. But in the light of the tragedy that had plunged us into a world holocaust, my job was no longer important."[56]

A letter to the General Executive Board is more frank about her resignation. She described her unresolvable conflict with Los Angeles vice president Louis Levy and concluded, "It is my firm belief that much of this could have been avoided if our President and Vice-President Levy had recognized the fact, that after nine years of service to our union, I was as competent as any of the men on our staff." She makes clear her loyalties to the Los Angeles rank and file, many of whom had written letters to national headquarters in support of her position. "I have the utmost confidence in their ability now to take care of themselves in any industrial struggle that they may have to face. They have stood the acid test of a major conflict. These workers—practically all women—are in the main Americans of old stock, whose forefathers have been in this county for generations. Many of them are former Dust-Bowlers, strong characters like Ma Joad and the other Okies now situated in the Pacific Coast. They have courage and native intelligence. They read our press, took it seriously, and know their rights under both the United States Constitution and the Constitution of the ILGWU."[57] Thousands of miles away in New York, Pesotta looked forward to joining other women of "courage and native intelligence" in the garment shops. By her own account, her idyllic workplace community was realized. In 1944, as her sister workers celebrated the publication of *Bread upon the Waters* with "speeches, drinks, laughter," she wrote, "I am feeling again at home—that I belong."[58] Four years later in the same spirit, she wrote, "The usual routine in the shop again. I worked feverishly till five the sweat running down my body and my forehead but strange as it may seem I was happy—that I was alive, healthy and vigorous to carry on."[59] Her diary suggests that Pesotta may have withdrawn from union office less for her stated political reasons than because she craved community and stability and found the need satisfied in New York's garment shops.

In 1944, Pesotta formally declined a fourth term on the General Executive Board. She told thousands of delegates assembled in Boston for the ILGWU's annual convention that her experience had proved "that a one woman vice-president could not adequately represent the women who now make up 85% of the International's membership of 305,000." She advised the union to take the rule of allowing only one woman on the General Executive Board and "throw it out the window." The bold critique of the union's sexism was not her last word, though. She tempered her statement by terming the one-woman rule an "unimportant subject" when compared with "a world aflame, with the democratic forces penetrating into the very heart of the Nazi fortress, with the day of liberation close at hand."[60]

Alice Kessler-Harris has written, "No one could question Pesotta's awareness of women's particular problems."[61] But neither Pesotta's awareness nor her personal resentment of her union brothers' sexism led her toward the feminist networks that supported ILGWU women like Pauline Newman and Rose Schneiderman. For Pesotta, class conflict, or the political issues of "a world aflame," always took precedence over women's issues. Her choice reflected in part her anarchist beliefs, in part the mixed-sex political and professional groups with which she associated, and in part, no doubt, the circumstances of her personal life.

Although she and Newman shared a common cultural background, Pesotta lived outside the woman-oriented community in which Newman spent most of her adult life. Pesotta was deeply involved with her extended family and found pleasure in dancing, nightclubs, and activities that made her feel "like a woman." Her romantic relationships tended to be passionate and often unhappy, alternating between periods of high elation and deep despair. She had numerous lovers, may have married twice, and had several affairs with married men.[62] The most important of her romances was a lengthy relationship with Powers Hapgood, whom she met during the Sacco-Vanzetti case. The relationship is documented in hundreds of letters that Hapgood sent Pesotta between 1936 and 1949.[63]

Powers Hapgood was like a crown prince of the Left. His uncles were Norman Hapgood, a progressive drama critic, and

Hutchins Hapgood, a writer, a reformer, and a close friend of Emma Goldman. Power's father, William, founded the Columbia Conserve Company, an experiment in industrial democracy. Like his father and uncles, Hapgood attended Harvard, where he found himself part of a radical circle influenced by the writings of Cornelia and Carleton Parker. Upon graduation, Hapgood "bummed around," rode the rails, and went to work as a miner. During the teens and early 1920s, Hapgood was in and out of jail while he helped organize foreign-born miners throughout the bituminous and anthracite coalfields. In 1926, he helped spearhead the ill-fated leftist challenge to John L. Lewis's presidency of the United Mine Workers. His role among the insurgents earned him prominence in the labor movement and Lewis's unenviable enmity. Essentially blackballed, he was unable to find work in the mines and eventually found a job with the Columbia Conserve Company in 1929. He returned to the labor movement in the 1930s as an organizer primarily for the Congress of Industrial Organization.

William Hapgood once accused his son of having more "'Hapgood egoism' than any one of us, except perhaps Uncle Hutch," and the comparison between the mercurial uncle and nephew seems apt.[64] In his books, "Uncle Hutch" wrote of the "authenticity" of Jewish life in New York's Lower East Side, of anarchist women, and of his own open marriage to writer Neith Boyce. Surely he would have looked with favor on his nephew's attraction to Rose Pesotta.

Like his uncle and other Hapgoods, Powers was an unstinting idealist. At eighteen, he wrote to his parents: "No matter at what age I go [die], I'll go happily if only I've completed or helped to complete some work which will permanently help the world. The tragedy of death, it seems to me is not in just the mere leaving of the earth and friends but the leaving of it before one has a chance to do something of value."[65]

It is easy to see how Hapgood and Pesotta could have been attracted to each other. Hapgood was Pesotta's equal in passion, energy, and commitment to the union cause. Surprisingly, since he had been at least a fellow traveler during the 1920s, he shared her antipathy toward Communists. She remembered him as "tall, husky and sun-tanned, handsome, earnestly smiling." He often addressed her as "my Rose of Akron"; they had first made love in Akron. With the drama and tension of a novel, their romance played itself out in the heady atmosphere of the labor wars of the 1930s.[66]

Pesotta detailed the affair's inception in a long and painful letter to Mary Donovan, Hapgood's wife and a comrade from the Sacco and Vanzetti Defense Committee.[67] She wrote of Hapgood's pursuit of her and her resistance along labor's trail in Akron, South Bend, Chicago, Homestead, and New York. She resolved to leave for Montreal, but at a meeting in Akron, "could not resist the persistent affections and the inevitable happened." She expressed "love and guilt" to Donovan and her hope that a "violent strike or something " would distract her from the affair. She concluded, "I do not know why I am writing you this, only to let you know how stupid we women are. Neither age nor experience is an assurance that we will not commit something foolish."[68] Why did Pesotta contact Donovan? Did she need forgiveness? Did her politics demand disclosure? Were shared feminine foibles intended to be the basis of a sisterly understanding? With nothing other than her letter to answer these questions, it is difficult to ascertain Pesotta's motivation. Clearly, though, she felt a sense of moral unease about her actions.

As Pesotta struggled with her guilt, Hapgood struggled to justify his own actions. In a letter that reads like a textbook account of an extramarital affair with leftist overlay, he wrote, "Oh, Rose, can't you see the difference between a man looking for sex affairs with any woman and a man have [sic] a real love for a person he admires. One is disloyalty, but the other is not. It would be disloyalty if I fell for a woman I had nothing in common with except sex desire and also it would be disloyalty if I deserted Mary and the kids for some one that I really loved, but I will never do either. Why should I hurt her by loving some one with the same nobility of character that she has and is tremendously beautiful, I can't understand."⁶⁹

In September he wrote of his consultation with Dr. Antoinette Konikov, "a comrade in the revolutionary movement." Told of his affair with Pesotta, the physician advised him not to have sex with his wife for six weeks, since even "fine" girls who had been with other men may have venereal disease.⁷⁰ Pesotta was furious. She became "positively hysterical" at the "mere thought of becoming the topic in [the Hapgood] household." Sarcastically, she urged Hapgood to tell Dr. Konikov and Mary "that we used very *hot water* with *boric acid*, liberally and in addition medicated alcohol rub. That's what any sensible person uses for her own protection—if she values her 'health.' "⁷¹ Perhaps to mollify her, he replied that he had told his parents of the affair but regretted having told Mary who his lover was. He claimed to be distraught enough to "rush for a bottle."

Hapgood's frequent rush for a bottle in fact complicated their affair as the relationship pursued a tender but tortured course through the 1930s that belies the buoyant tone of *Bread upon the Waters*. Pesotta wrote from Montreal that she wanted to avoid New York and proximity to him, but "I am leading a most drearly [*sic*] life here with practically no friends nor social life. . . . We are doing a lot of work, but it does not satisfy me at all."⁷² Pesotta's trysts with Hapgood assuaged her restlessness. The relationship took the edge off the acute loneliness that was a persistent feature of her organizing trips. On a deeper level, too, Pesotta had found a soulmate in Hapgood. Each confident of the other's sympathetic and knowledgeable response, they exchanged long letters describing daily life in the field and the Byzantine politics of the labor movement. For about five years they were partners in a dance, sometimes together but at other times thrust apart by Hapgood's bouts with alcoholism and Pesotta's battles with guilt.

The time they spent together was filled with romantic walks, dancing, and dinners. When they were separated, their letters crossed America almost daily. They wrote of labor and politics, but they also wrote of books read and movies seen, of families and friends. In 1938, Hapgood ordered *Bakunin* as a gift for his anarchist lover but first read it himself, anticipating her pleasure. He urged her to see *Arise, My Love*; its backdrop of the Spanish Civil War would please her. She suggested *Cheers for Miss Bishop*. With the onset of the Second World War, each struggled with isolationist sentiments. In this war, Hapgood reasoned, Hitler killed labor activists, liberals, radicals, suppressed minorities, and Jews.

Hapgood's alcoholism cast a dark shadow across the relationship. His bouts with "drink" left him feeling guilty and angered Pesotta. She sent him articles and books and urged him to go into treatment. After one incident she claimed it would be "impossible" for her to see him again unless he got help. She warned, "If you want to retain your position in the Labor Movement and your name in the REVOLUTIONARY movement you will, you must, get cured. You are now very sick Powers, and perhaps you do not know it, but we who are close to you get sick ourselves after we see how you are killing yourself."⁷³ At times Pesotta's relationship to Hapgood seemed maternal; at other times she seemed to play the older, wiser sibling to Hapgood's junior, particularly when the subject was alcohol. For a time they had a contract, renewable annually, that Pesotta would continue to see him if he moderated his drinking. As their meetings became less frequent, Pesotta could monitor his drinking less carefully. At a 1944 convention she expressed shock at his appearance and "fed him a good breakfast." Soon afterward she wrote him a letter expressing concern about his "mental condition." She urged a "complete change of environment for him" and suggested that he hire displaced workers from the Southern Tenants Farmers Union for his farm. She reminded him that he "was too young and valuable a labor leader to be wasted away. There is still a job to be done, the younger people need alert leadership from the ranks, and no one could do a better job than you." She urged him to "stop this excessive drinking, go to a physician . . . And please try to drink milk, it is good for babys [*sic*] and for grown ups (meaning babys like yourself)."⁷⁴

He acknowledged her feelings of guilt about their extramarital affair but claimed not to share them. As he wrote in 1937, "I really believed in the teachings of Bertrad [*sic*] Russell and Havelock Ellis long before I followed them. Apparently I have chosen almost the only two vigorous women I know who don't believe them, you and Mary."[75]

By 1941, the passion seemed spent, and the relationship evolved into a caring friendship. As friends they shared the idealism of their generation of organizers, an idealism that Pesotta found lacking in the 1940s. Writing to Hapgood, she recalled their glory days and noted: "We are entering a new era—the era of arbitration by disinterested individuals mostly on government payroll, who will consider this some times as an unpleasant duty while the workers will remain aloof, the leaders will disclaim any responsibility, and thus the old labor movement will die a natural death."[76]

Hapgood died in an automobile accident on a snowy winter road in 1949. Pesotta in her tribute to him wrote of "an idealist of purest, rarest quality . . . a crusader for human rights . . . who never did things half-way."[77] To her diary she confided, "I shall miss his fellowship," and at his funeral she was "the only one who did not hide the tears."[78]

It appears that Pesotta's anarchist belief in "free unions" did little to assuage her pain in relationships with Hapgood and other men. She spent days in tearful depressions and often called herself a "loser." Once she blamed Hapgood for making her "an old maid." He replied, "Darling, if there was anyone you loved I wouldn't stand in the way."[79]

Pesotta's affair with Hapgood invites comparisons with Emma Goldman's passionate romance with Ben Reitman.[80] Both anarchist women began their relationships when they were almost forty, an age when Goldman, Alice Wexler tells us, was "becoming increasingly aware of the difficulty of being an independent woman. Despite her own success, she felt her life painfully incomplete."[81] Both found the Americanness of their lovers attractive, and both cast themselves in their relationships as "the subordinate, suffering partner."[82] Just as Pesotta longed for a "violent strike" that would allow her to sublimate her desire for Hapgood, so too did Goldman write to Reitman of "Activity, propaganda. That is my salvation. . . . That is the only force which reconciles me to my mad passion for you."[83]

Perhaps even more deeply than Pesotta, Goldman believed in and wrote extensively about the anarchist creed of free unions. At first glance, her stirring words about sexual libertarianism seem at variance with the dependence that characterized her relationship with Reitman. Her biographer reminds us, though, that we never become truly detached from our historical context. "Goldman acted out in a highly dramatic fashion the contradictory values experienced by many women at this moment of transition from the Victorian era to the modern: the conflict between masochistic nineteenth-century values of self-sacrifice, submission, and dependence associated with the ideal of 'true womanhood' and the modern values of assertion, self-expression, and independence associated with the 'new woman' of the early twentieth century."[84] Much the same could be said of Pesotta. Like Goldman, she embraced anarchist sentiments about sexuality and relationships, but emotionally she longed for the security of more conventional arrangements.[85]

Soon after Pesotta returned to the shops, she began work on *Bread upon the Waters* with the help of John Nicholas Beffel, a labor journalist. The memoir covers the years from 1933 to 1944, when Pesotta was an ILGWU organizer and vice president. In the book Pesotta characterizes herself as a brilliant strategist, a charismatic speaker, and an indefatigable worker. She emerges in *Bread upon the Waters* as one of labor's most valuable assets during this period.[86]

In *Bread upon the Waters*, too, Pesotta presented herself as an American. The metaphor of an airplane trip framed her introduction. As she flew deeper into the heart of America, traveling from union headquarters in New York to her organizing task in Los Angeles, she reflected on her journey from Russia several decades earlier. Landings at Harrisburg, Pittsburgh, Chicago, Kansas

City, Amarillo, and Albuquerque punctuated memories of milestones in her transition from the shtetl to union organizing in the New World.

Despite the central role that anarchism played in Pesotta's life, she never calls her philosophy by name in *Bread upon the Waters*. But her repeated tales of grassroots organizing, building a union culture, and using the union to meet the social problems of workers and their families all resonate with the anarchist concept of the trade union. Her repeated emphasis on the multicultural and international constituency of the labor movement—Puerto Ricans, French Canadians, Mexican Americans—drew attention to the potential for an inclusive, international workers' movement. She deftly created for her readers a vision of labor that was broad, triumphant, and patriotic.[87]

Bread upon the Waters was remarkably successful. Although there were objections to Pesotta's critical assessment of union officials in Los Angeles, many readers responded to Pesotta's exuberant portrayal of labor organizing in the 1930s. The book quickly went into a third printing and was translated into Japanese, Spanish, and German. She had originally hoped that it would "be received favorably by the working people." In the end, she wrote to Hapgood, it was to her "just as important as to Roosevelt to be re-elected."[88]

Riding the crest of her fame in August 1945, Pesotta accepted a job with the B'nai B'rith Anti-Defamation League. For about a year she traveled extensively, speaking to labor groups about prejudice and discrimination. In 1946, Haakon Lie, secretary general of the Norwegian labor party, invited Pesotta to address the International Labor Institute in Sormarka on the labor situation in the United States. From Norway, Pesotta went on to Sweden and then to the ravaged areas of Eastern Europe. In Poland, which she called one vast Jewish cemetery, she visited Lublin Maidanek concentration camp and made contact with members of the Bund, the Jewish Socialist Party. A train ride evoked memories of her father accompanying her across Poland to the German border in 1913 for her trip to America. Others on the train stared as she spoke Yiddish to her companion. She imagined them thinking, "Watch these Jews. They are still alive, and they dare to show themselves among decent people again."[89]

The trip powerfully reinforced Pesotta's Jewishness. She had always identified herself as a Jew, although her appearance and name led her often to be taken for Italian or Spanish.[90] At a testimonial dinner held before she left Los Angeles in 1942, she condemned anti-Semitic propaganda with the words "I AM A JEW! I was born in a good Hebrew family and have made my contribution to society as well as anyone present in this hall! I have no apologies to offer anyone nor am I ashamed of my nationality! Some of the greatest minds have been born of the same race and have made their contribution to the human welfare."[91]

The war renewed Pesotta's sense of herself as a Jew. It also inspired in her memories of her youth and in her mind established Judaism, especially its embodiment in the state of Israel, as a cause. Upon her return from Europe she immediately set to work on two books, one, *The Jew Is Human, Too*, a novel loosely based on her family, and the other an account of the labor situation in Europe. Neither book found a publisher.

Her next attempts at fiction were two novels, *From My Left-Hand Pocket* and *The Unconquerables*, which she never completed. *From My Left-Hand Pocket* tells of a young Yeshiva student who initiates a sexual relationship with the daughter of a beadle. When the girl's mother discovers the young couple in her bed, the young man is banished. His lover follows him only to find that he has fallen in love with someone else.

The Unconquerables or *Family Album* begins with the Nuremberg trials and flashes back to follow the fortunes, decades earlier, of a Jewish family loosely patterned on the Pesoitys. Pesotta's stories lacked the critical tone of Anzia Yezierska or the social realism of Michael Gold. Their sentimentality made them more akin to Shalom Aleichem's nostalgic stories of Russia.

Pesotta found a more authentic voice for her experiences in nonfictional autobiography. Between 1950 and 1957 she wrote her coming-of-age memoir, *Days of Our Lives*. Like another autobiography of a radical woman, Agnes Smedley's *Daughter of Earth*, *Days of Our Lives* tried to answer the bildungsroman question, "how I came to be who I am." Unlike Smedley, though, Pesotta in her reply created a near-perfect family, noble parents, and a warm Jewish community. At first glance, it seems odd that Pesotta made Judaism prominent in her memoir after a lifetime spent in secular activism and outside the family role so critical to Jewish practice. Closer scrutiny, however, shows that Pesotta's idealized past laid the foundation for her American life. *Days of Our Lives* makes clear the importance of Pesotta's father as an influence on her. Although her mother was a model of female autonomy, her father articulated the values of equality and social responsibility that animated her later life. The unique "interlinguistic and bicultural" world of the Russian Pale and the "external power relationships" to which Jews in Tsarist Russia were subjected prefigured the Jewish labor union in tension with a dominant culture. And of course Pesotta notes that her adolescent political activity exerted a formative influence. As Virginia Yans-McLaughlin reminds us, Eastern European Jews frequently participated in political movements that were compatible with "modern notions of history because they assumed the possibility that human action could bring about change in this world."[92] In a sense, then, Derazhnya came to America: the union was an extended family, the employers and their company goons like Cossacks, and the workers comparable to the simple, honest peasants in *Days of Our Lives*.

About some areas of Pesotta's life, though, *Days of Our Lives* is silent. We learn of her strenuous objection to a conventional marriage, while we know from her flirtatious behavior on the trip to America that she enjoyed male attention. And there are few clues to the mystery of her often painful adult personal life. Emma Goldman speaks of a troubled family of origin and a father who preferred sons, a history that might interfere with the search for love in later life, but the description of an idyllic family in *Days of Our Lives* offers no comparable evidence. Perhaps Pauline Newman is more nearly similar. Both Newman and Pesotta do not discuss their private matters in their autobiographies, yet both amply document their intimate relationships in their bequests to archives. It is as if they were declining to interpret their personal lives themselves but were inviting others to do so.[93]

At about the time that she began her second memoir, Pesotta took a position with the American Trade Union Council for Histadrut, the labor organization of Israel, as midwest director based in Chicago.[94] Although she had turned down other offers to do union work, the combination of labor and Israel in Histadrut seemed irresistible. Doing what she did best, she traveled around the country speaking in support of Israel and fund-raising for Histadrut. Her invaluable union contacts opened doors for her appeal. Unions as well as individual unionists contributed to what Pesotta regarded as a noble social experiment similar to that which had been conducted in Spain in the 1930s.[95] American labor, however, seemed uninterested in Israel during the postwar years, and by 1950 Histadrut in the United States had become a part of the United Jewish Appeal. Pesotta herself seemed to feel some of the same ambivalence toward the organization that she experienced in the labor movement. After a Histadrut conference in 1949, she commented, "I feel sort of not belonging—they do not recognize employees. . . . am determined not to stay on too long as a cog in their machine."[96]

In March she resigned from the organization, and in April and May of 1950, Pesotta visited Israel to see the new world for herself.[97] With her characteristic energy, she tried to sample every aspect of Israeli life. She traveled all over the country, visiting hospitals, unions, kibbutzes, and parliament. She wrote approvingly of Israel's democratic government and joined the lively political discourse she heard all around her. Like many American Jews, she returned to the United States more eager than ever to support the Jewish state.[98]

Pesotta never took another professional job with a Jewish organization, though. Instead she returned to the place where she had always felt she most belonged. Between 1950 and 1965 she worked at the Will Stenman Dress Company in New York, where she found fellowship among a "miniature United Nations" of women.[99]

She continued to be active in the Women's Division of the Jewish Labor Committee, which raised funds for refugees and supported civil rights. She never ceased to identify with anarchism. She served as a member of the advisory board of the Libertarian Book Club and gave an annual address at a memorial for Sacco and Vanzetti.

Like Dreier and Newman, Pesotta lived to see the beginnings of another era of social reform. She joined her union local in the 1963 March on Washington and heard Martin Luther King voice his dream of a more just and equal society. His were the goals she herself had worked a lifetime to achieve.

In the fall of 1965, she was diagnosed with cancer of the spleen. Quietly she resigned from her job and went to Miami to "recuperate in the sun." On 4 December she died alone in a Miami hospital. Five days later 400 friends and colleagues crowded a New York funeral chapel to pay their respects to this "woman warrior" and "rebel girl." ILGWU vice president Gus Tyler noted that she had always experienced conflict as a "born leader and innate rank and filer . . . , one to whom workers turned as an authority, while she held fast to the anarchist distrust of all authority." Tyler concluded, "She was like a torch that ignited whatever she touched."[100]

Such tributes failed to acknowledge the tensions Pesotta experienced as a woman in a male-dominated profession and as a single woman in a world where marriage was the norm. Pesotta lived life without a script. Few women had demanding union careers, and few single women had heterosexual relationships outside marriage. The Bund heroines and Emma Goldman, whom Pesotta emulated, were models ill suited to a single woman seeking to construct a satisfying life in mid-twentieth-century America. She had internalized the prevailing social sense of what was appropriate for women to such a degree that she called herself a loser.

She was, of course, far from being a loser. She had enlisted thousands of women in a union that significantly improved the quality of life for them and their families. She inspired young women she encountered in Puerto Rico, Montreal, Los Angeles, and other cities; she set a standard as an independent woman. She repeatedly forced the world's largest union of woman workers to confront its sexism and its bigotry. Her family and friends mourned her passing.

While Pesotta was as deeply distressed by social inequality as Barnum, Dreier, and Newman, and as passionately committed to social justice, she differed from them in her community, her sexuality, and her politics. But her life, like those of my other three subjects, was rich in ambiguity and complexity. Politically she flew anarchism's banner until the end of her life, yet she worked with trade unions and hoped for a government appointment during the 1940s. Anarchism provided community as well as an ethical orientation for Pesotta. As she traveled worldwide, she sought out anarchist "comrades" for companionship. But the Black, Jewish, and Italian workers who peopled New York's garment shops were Pesotta's community as well. During many lonely hours on the road, she longed to return to the warmth and solidarity of the shops.

Pesotta's attraction to men, and her affairs with various colleagues and comrades, made her an unlikely candidate for the homosocial circles of women reformers that included Barnum, Dreier, and Newman. While she resented sexism and cared for women workers as much as they did, she believed that a better future for workers, both women and men, lay with the labor movement.

One could make the case that Pesotta's decision in 1942 to resign her vice presidency and return to the shops pitted her desire for personal happiness against her political goals. After all, could she not have accomplished more for women workers as an organizer and a role model by remaining a union official than she could as a worker? Yet her years in the shop gave her the opportunity to write her hugely successful *Bread upon the Waters*, which told her readership what one woman could do.

The tragedy of her life was twofold. Her tempestuous romances failed to fulfill her youthful romantic goals, and this failure at times blocked her own appreciation of her many accomplishments. And the union whose faults she could see so clearly ignored her pleas for greater awareness of, and responsiveness to, its female and multiethnic membership. In doing so, it lost the services of one of its most talented leaders.

By contrast with Newman, Pesotta entered the labor movement at a time when the drama of the Uprising of the 20,000 and the Triangle fire had become the stuff of myth and legend. Her extensive background in worker education meant that she brought a systematic approach to her organizing, and when she arrived in a unfamiliar city, she was usually greeted by at least a skeleton union staff. The support of the New Deal for industrial unionism cannot be underestimated. Pesotta was a propagandist in settings primed for her message. She shared with Newman the concept of the union as a welfare organization as well as the burden of its sexism. But where Newman found her feminism reinforced in her personal life, Pesotta lacked the support of like-minded women.

Shortly before her death, Pesotta expressed the ideals that had animated her activist life: "I've been asked—what if you could live life over—I have no regrets of my chosen path of the past. I would choose the same path, trying perhaps to avoid some of the mistakes of the past. But always having the vision before me in the words of Thomas Paine, 'The world is my country. To do good is my religion.'"[101]

CONCLUSION

By the 1990s, eighty years after Gertrude Barnum had published her hopeful vision of wage work for women, much of the promise of "The Pig-Headed Girl" seemed fulfilled. The majority of American women worked outside the home and had made significant inroads into the major professions and politics. The creator of the spunky turn-of-the-century working girl might marvel at the technological advances of the late twentieth century but would surely have applauded women's visibility as television news anchors and astronauts. Slightly more women than men were enrolled in colleges and universities, and although gender wage differentials still existed, the gap appeared to be closing.

Yet, however fully we can see the progress made by working women since the years when Barnum, Dreier, Newman, and Pesotta were activists, we must acknowledge the troubling conditions that remain. Just as the Triangle Shirtwaist fire made the sweatshop into front page news in 1911, so did the grounding of the ship *Golden Venture* in the summer of 1992 draw attention to a shocking and extensive world of illegal immigration and profoundly exploitative working conditions. One need only walk in New York's Chinatown at dusk and see lights on the upper floors of tenements to understand that the sweatshop is once again alive and well in the very neighborhoods where it flourished eighty years ago. There Asian women—and their Hispanic counterparts in Los Angeles—work long hours in unregulated conditions little different from the factories investigated by Mary Dreier, Pauline Newman, and Rose Pesotta.

Moreover, despite the ubiquity of women's wage work in the United States, debates persist about women's appropriate social role. Studies have shown that most American women work a "double day" and bear primary responsibility for child care and household chores in addition to their jobs. By 1960, 18.6 percent of married women with children under six years old worked outside the home, but by 1992, economic need had drawn almost 60 percent of this cohort into the workforce. Work for these women, in particular, has come to mean not liberation and self-actualization but rather a nightmare as they struggle with inadequate and expensive childcare and with the demands of full-time employment.

If Barnum, Dreier, Newman, and Pesotta were to survey the state of the working woman today with their activist eyes, what conclusions would they draw, what solutions would they advocate, in what political direction would they move? The Women's Trade Union League is no more. Suffrage is long won, and by 1970 feminists and the labor movement both had voiced their support for the Equal Rights Amendment. American anarchists today are few and far between. The collapse of the Soviet Union has generated fresh criticism of socialism. The welfare state, with its programs of protection for women and children, seems as I write, about to collapse or to be dismantled. And the labor movement, with a leadership still dominated by white men, represents fewer than 20 percent of American workers and fewer than 15 percent of women workers.

Yet American trade unions continue to offer the greatest potential for realizing the ideals of social justice espoused by Barnum, Dreier, Newman, and Pesotta. Trade unions are democratic organizations that can, it has been shown, respond to the concerns of a progressive membership. Women are a permanent part of the labor force, and unions can address their concerns about child care, health care, sexual harassment, and a range of other issues if women organize and participate. Moreover, the global market in goods, labor, and ideas that the labor movement currently finds so troubling can unite rather than divide workers if the labor movement seeks to realize its global potential, cooperates with international unions, and insists on the presence of organized labor in the developing world.

Finally, we need new stories and new narratives. Barnum, Dreier, Newman, and Pesotta fought for and celebrated the fulfillment and sense of community afforded by women's work. We have lost sight of the way in which work and education opened the path to full citizenship for women and have felt too heavily the burden rather than the possibilities of work. While no one wants to make a career of a sweatshop, renewed activism can improve working conditions and can help realize the dignity that my four subjects struggled to find in work for women.

NOTES

INTRODUCTION

1. Gertrude Barnum, "The Pig-Headed Girl," *Ladies' Garment Worker* 3 (April 1912): 26–27.

2. Bill Shepard is quoted in Leon Stein, *The Triangle Fire* (Philadelphia, 1972), 20.

3. Susan A. Glenn, *Daughters of the Shtetl: Life and Labor in the Immigrant Generation* (Ithaca, N.Y., 1990); Sarah Eisenstein, *Give Us Bread but Give Us Roses: Working Women's Consciousness in the United States, 1890 to the First World War* (London and Boston, 1983).

4. Historians who claim that Jewish women's identity was still primarily based on their family roles are: Sydney Weinberg, *World of Our Mothers* (Chapel Hill, N.C., 1988), and Elizabeth Ewen, *Immigrant Women in the Land of Dollars: Life and Culture on the Lower East Side, 1890–1925* (New York, 1985).

5. Regina Morantz-Sanchez, *Sympathy and Science: Women Physicians in American Medicine* (New York, 1985); Rosalind Rosenberg *Beyond Separate Spheres: Intellectual Roots of Modern Feminism* (New Haven, Conn., 1982); Dee Garrison, *Apostles of Culture: The Public Librarian and American Society, 1876–1920* (New York, 1979).

6. Kathryn Kish Sklar, "Hull House in the 1890s: A Community of Woman Reformers," *Signs* 10 (Summer 1985): 658–77. Allen F. Davis, *Spear-*

heads for Reform: The Social Settlements and the Progressive Movement, 1890–1914 (New York, 1967); Rivka Shpak Lissak, *Pluralism and Progressives: Hull House and the New Immigrant, 1890–1919* (Chicago, 1989); Kathryn Kish Sklar, *Florence Kelley and the Nation's Work: The Rise of Women's Political Culture, 1830–1900* (New Haven, 1995).

7. Alice Kessler-Harris, "Independence and Virtue in the Lives of Wage-Earning Women in the United States, 1870–1930," in *Women in Culture and Politics: A Century of Change*, ed. Judith Friedlander et al. (Bloomington, Ind., 1986): 3–17. Kessler-Harris goes on to suggest that the tension between virtue and independence was not resolved until the 1920s, when "socially ordained roles at home gave way for the first time to an unapologetic notion of work for individual satisfaction," 5.

8. For a discussion of Dreier and Newman's motivations, see Ann Schofield, " 'To Do and To Be': Mary Dreier, Pauline Newman, and the Psychology of Feminist Activism," *Psychohistory Review* 18 (December 1989): 33–55.

9. Nancy F. Cott, *The Grounding of Modern Feminism* (New Haven, 1987), 13. Regarding women's public activism, Cott suggests that we look at three aspects of consciousness: feminism, female consciousness ("a mind-set not biologically female but socially constructed from women's common tasks"), and communal consciousness ("based on solidarity with men and women of the same group").

10. William L. O'Neill, *Everyone Was Brave: The Rise and Fall of Feminism in America* (Chicago, 1969). O'Neill divided feminists into categories of "social" and "hard-core" and saw these as mutually exclusive terms, the first referring to women who envisioned suffrage as a method for gaining broader social reforms, the latter denoting women committed exclusively to achieving women's rights. J. Stanley Lemons reinforced O'Neill's terminology and applied the categories specifically to the 1920s in *The Woman Citizen: Social Feminism in the 1920s* (Urbana, Ill., 1973).

11. Nancy F. Cott, "What's in a Name? The Limits of 'Social Feminism'; or, Expanding the Vocabulary of Women's History," *Journal of American History* 76 (December 1989): 809–29.

12. Cott, "What's in a Name?" 819.

13. Dorothy Sue Cobble, " 'Practical Women': Waitress Unionists and the Controversies over Gender Roles in the Food Service Industry, 1900–1980," *Labor History* 29 (Winter 1988): 5–31.

14. Mildred Moore, "A History of the Women's Trade Union League of Chicago" (master's thesis, University of Chicago, 1915), 3, cited in Diane Kirkby, *Alice Henry: The Power of Pen and Voice: The Life of an Australian-American Labor Reformer* (Cambridge, 1991), 29. Eventually the WTUL agenda embodied " 'industrial feminism' which, influenced by Fabian socialist views of state intervention, linked organization, education and legislation." Kirkby, *Alice Henry*, 133, 147.

15. Ellen Carol DuBois, "Working Women, Class Relations, and Suffrage

Militance: Harriet Stanton Blatch and the New York Suffrage Movement, 1894–1909," *Journal of American History* 74 (June 1987): 34–58 (quoted passage on p. 40).

16. Aileen S. Kraditor, *The Ideas of the Woman Suffrage Movement, 1890–1920* (New York, 1971).

17. Pauline M. Newman, "We Are Tired of Asking You Men," n.d., Pauline M. Newman Papers, Arthur and Elizabeth Schlesinger Library, Radcliffe College, Cambridge, Mass. (hereafter cited as PMN papers). Ellen DuBois writes of the tightrope that militant suffragists had to walk in dealing with socialists: "Militants could neither repudiate the Socialist support they were attracting, and alienate working-class women, nor associate too closely with Socialists and lose access to the wealthy." DuBois, "Working Women," 57.

18. DuBois, "Working Women."

19. DuBois, "Working Women."

20. DuBois, "Working Women."

21. Nancy Schrom Dye, *As Equals and as Sisters: Feminism, Unionism, and the Women's Trade Union League of New York* (Columbia, Mo., 1980); Elizabeth Anne Payne, *Reform, Labor, and Feminism: Margaret Dreier Robins and the Women's Trade Union League* (Urbana, Ill., 1988); Alice Kessler-Harris, *Out to Work: A History of Wage-Earning Women in the United States* (New York, 1982); Sarah Eisenstein, *Give Us Bread but Give Us Roses: Working Women's Consciousness in the United States, 1890 to the First World War* (London and Boston, 1983); Diane Kirkby, *Alice Henry.*

22. Eisenstein, *Give Us Bread*, 10, 150.

23. Payne, *Reform, Labor*, 4. On the end of women's political culture, see also Paula Baker, "The Domestication of Politics: Women and American Political Society, 1780–1920," *American Historical Review* 89 (June 1984): 620–49. This book will take issue with that view; I contend that the lives of these activists demonstrate that a female political culture continued well into the twentieth century. It is useful to ask whether we can securely generalize about the League given the differing views of its leaders. Diane Kirkby disputes Nancy Schrom Dye's assertion that the League began as a labor organization and soon became a reform organization. Kirkby defines the WTUL from its inception as a "women's reform organization." She goes on, though, to note that Alice Henry voiced wholehearted support for state intervention. By contrast, Margaret Dreier Robins took an "antistatist" position and complained that the New Deal had betrayed the American tradition of voluntarism.

24. "Civic maternalism" is a term that has emerged from a burgeoning body of scholarship on women and the welfare state. This scholarship includes: Linda Gordon, ed., *Women, the State, and Welfare* (Madison, 1990); Sonya Michel and Seth Koven, "Womanly Duties: Maternalist Politics and the Origins of Welfare States in France, Germany, Great Britain, and the United States, 1880–1920," *American Historical Review* 95 (October 1990): 1076–

1108; Theda Skocpol, *Protecting Soldiers and Mothers: The Political Origins of Social Policy in the United States* (Cambridge, Mass., 1992); Mimi Abramovitz, *Regulating the Lives of Women: Social Welfare Policy from Colonial Times to the Present* (Boston, 1988); Linda Gordon, "Social Insurance and Public Assistance: The Influence of Gender in Welfare Thought in the United States, 1890–1935," *American Historical Review* 97 (February 1992): 19–54; and Seth Koven and Sonya Michel, eds., *Mothers of a New World: Maternalist Politics and the Origins of Welfare States* (New York, 1993). See also Eileen Boris's comments in "Women's Welfare," *Nation* (22 April 1991): 526–28.

25. Newman, unlike native-born women socialists, whose participation in politics was shaped by the cultural experience of separate spheres, participated in mixed-sex locals. When speaking under the socialist banner, she always cast the demand for suffrage in terms of the class struggle. Mari Jo Buhle, *Women and American Socialism, 1870–1920* (Urbana, Ill., 1981), identifies a genuine socialist women's movement, with its own magazines, agenda, and rituals. On socialist feminism, see 290ff.

26. Between 1905 and 1915, mass strikes of female garment workers had varying degrees of success in New York, Rochester, Chicago, and Cleveland. For a discussion of these strikes, see Joan M. Jensen and Sue Davidson, eds., *A Needle, A Bobbin, A Strike: Women Needleworkers in America* (Philadelphia, 1984), 81–182.

27. Founded in 1914, the Amalgamated Clothing Workers of America organized in the men's clothing trade and shared many characteristics with the ILGWU.

28. Blanche Wiesen Cook, *Eleanor Roosevelt, Volume 1: 1884–1933* (New York, 1992).

29. Peter Gay has challenged some of the formulations of feminist historians in his four-volume work: *Education of the Senses: Victoria to Freud* (New York, 1984), *The Tender Passion* (New York, 1986), *The Cultivation of Hatred* (New York, 1993), and *The Naked Heart* (New York, 1995).

30. Susan Ware, *Partner and I: Molly Dewson, Feminism, and New Deal Politics* (New Haven, Conn., 1987).

31. Barbara Sicherman, *Alice Hamilton: A Life in Letters* (Cambridge, Mass., 1984).

32. Other comparative biographies include: Ellen Condliffe Lagemann, *A Generation of Women: Education in the Lives of Progressive Reformers* (Cambridge, Mass., 1979); Barbara Caine, *Victorian Feminists* (New York, 1992); Ellen Fitzpatrick, *Endless Crusade: Women Social Scientists and Progressive Reform* (New York, 1992); Annelise Orleck, *Common Sense and a Little Fire: Women and Working Class Politics in the United States, 1900–1965* (Chapel Hill, N.C., 1995); Susan Ware, *Beyond Suffrage: Women in the New Deal* (Cambridge, Mass., 1981).

1. Gertrude Barnum to Fannia Cohn, 23 June 1945, subject file B, box 1, Archives of the International Ladies' Garment Workers' Union, New York School of Industrial and Labor Relations, Cornell University, Ithaca, N.Y.

2. Paula Baker, "The Domestication of Politics: Women and American Political Society, 1780–1920," *American Historical Review* 89 (June 1984): 620–49; Kathryn Kish Sklar, "The Historical Foundations of Women's Power in the Creation of the American Welfare State, 1890–1930," in *Mothers of a New World: Maternalist Politics and the Origins of Welfare States*, ed. Seth Koven and Sonya Michel (New York, 1993), 43–93; on women's separate political culture, see also Estelle Freedman, "Separatism as Strategy: Female Institution Building, 1870–1930," *Feminist Studies* 5 (Fall 1979): 512–29; Elisabeth Israels Perry, *Belle Moskowitz: Feminine Politics and the Exercise of Power in the Age of Alfred E. Smith* (New York, 1987); Kathryn Kish Sklar, "Hull House in the 1890s: A Community of Woman Reformers," *Signs* 10 (Summer 1985): 658–77; Linda Gordon, ed., *Women, the State, and Welfare* (Madison, 1990); Seth Koven and Sonya Michel, "Womanly Duties: Maternalist Politics and the Origins of Welfare States in France, Germany, Great Britain, and the United States, 1880–1920," *American Historical Review* 95 (October 1990): 1076–1108.

3. Sklar, "Hull House in the 1890s," 663.

4. Allen F. Davis and Mary Lynn McCree, eds., *Eighty Years at Hull House* (Chicago, 1969), 5.

5. Sklar, "Hull House in the 1890s," 663.

6. Hull House when Jane Addams first saw it was "a fine old house standing well back from the street, surrounded on three sides by a broad piazza which was supported by wooden pillars of exceptionally pure Corinthian design." Jane Addams, *Twenty Years at Hull House* (New York, 1910), quoted in Davis and McCree, *Eighty Years*, 25. By 1907 Hull House comprised thirteen buildings. Also see Rivka Shpak Lissak, *Pluralism and Progressives: Hull House and the New Immigrants, 1890–1919* (Chicago, 1989).

7. Davis and McCree, *Eighty Years*, 23.

8. Quoted in Davis and McCree, *Eighty Years*, 7.

9. Observers disagreed about the type of social interaction that took place between male and female residents. Dorothea Moore, writing in 1897, replied to a visitor's question, "Do they marry?" with "Often, alas, often" (quoted in Davis and McCree, *Eighty Years*, 52–58). Abraham Bisno, a labor organizer and a frequent visitor, claimed, however: "These people seldom sing, almost never dance, and their attitude toward each other carries no sign of their sex life" (quoted in Davis and McCree, *Eighty Years*, 21).

10. Dorothea Moore, "A Day at Hull House," *American Journal of Sociology* 2 (March 1897): 629–40, excerpted in Davis and McCree, *Eighty Years*, 52–58.

11. School extension was for students with at least six years of schooling.

12. *Hull House Bulletin*, 13 January 1896.

13. Hull House also maintained a Bureau of Labor headed by Florence Kelley and funded by the Chicago Women's Club. Sklar, "The Historical Foundation," 15.

14. *Hull House Bulletin*, 15 October 1896.

15. "The Reminiscences of Frances Perkins" (1955), Oral History Collection, Columbia University, New York.

16. Ibid., 9ff.

17. Jane Addams to Mary Rozet Smith, 23 February 1897, Jane Addams Papers, Swarthmore College, Swarthmore, Pa.

18. Madeline Sikes to her mother, 22 September 1896, 1 October 1896, Madeline Sikes Papers, Chicago Historical Society, Chicago, Ill. I am grateful to Louise Wilbey Knight for this reference. On the conflict between marriage and a career for women of the Progressive Era, see Rosalind Rosenberg, *Beyond Separate Spheres: Intellectual Roots of Modern Feminism* (New Haven, Conn., 1982), and Ellen Fitzpatrick, *Endless Crusade: Women Social Scientists and Progressive Reform* (New York, 1990).

19. Kathryn Kish Sklar, "Hull House in the 1890s," 663.

20. "Henry Booth House," in Robert A. Woods and Albert J. Kennedy, *Handbook of Settlements* (New York, 1911).

21. Gertrude Barnum in *Weekly Bulletin of the Clothing Trades* 24 (March 1905): 2, quoted in Nancy Schrom Dye, *As Equals and as Sisters: Feminism, Unionism, and the Women's Trade Union League of New York* (Columbia, Mo., 1980), 41–42.

22. "The Reminiscences of Frances Perkins" (1955), Oral History Collection, Columbia University.

23. Tension between the sexes is well documented in histories of women and the U.S. labor movement such as Philip S. Foner, *Women and the American Labor Movement*, 2 vols. (New York, 1979–80); and Alice Kessler-Harris, *Out to Work: A History of Wage-Earning Women in the United States* (New York, 1982).

24. Histories of the Women's Trade Union League include: Nancy Schrom Dye, *As Equals and as Sisters: Feminism, Unionism, and the Women's Trade Union League of New York* (Columbia, Mo., 1980); Elizabeth Anne Payne, *Reform, Labor, and Feminism: Margaret Dreier Robins and the Women's Trade Union League* (Urbana, Ill., 1988); Robin Miller Jacoby, "The Women's Trade Union League and American Feminism," in *Class, Sex, and the Woman Worker*, ed. Milton Cantor and Bruce Laurie (Westport, Conn., 1977): 203–24.

25. Minutes of the Executive Board, Papers of the New York Women's Trade Union League, New York State Labor Library, New York, 28 July, 29 September, 25 August; and Rheta Childe Dorr, "The Women Strikers of Troy," *Charities* 15 (1905): 233–36. Dorr's autobiography portrays a free-

spirited feminist who divorced her husband and supported herself and her son as a newspaperwoman and a writer for popular magazines. She wrote frequently about the suffrage and labor reform causes. Rheta Childe Dorr, *A Woman of Fifty* (1924; reprint, New York 1980).

26. Gertrude Barnum, "Button, Button Who's Got the Button?" *Survey* (1911). During the Great Uprising of garment workers in New York in 1911, Barnum visited Mayor Gaynor to request protection for "girl strikers" against "white slave procurers." Gaynor replied, "There is no white slave traffic in New York."

27. Sklar discusses the support given women's activism by the importance of public opinion in the Progressive Era. See Sklar, "The Historical Foundations." On this same topic, Sklar cites Richard L. McCormick, *From Realignment to Reform: Political Change in New York State, 1893–1910* (Ithaca, N.Y., 1981).

28. *Cleveland Press*, reprinted in the *Ladies' Garment Worker* 2 (December 1911): 4, quoted in Lois Scharf, "The Great Uprising in Cleveland: When Sisterhood Failed," in *A Needle, A Bobbin, A Strike: Women Needleworkers in America*, ed. Joan Jensen and Sue Davidson (Philadelphia, 1984), 146.

29. Pauline Newman to Rose Schneiderman, 14 November 1911, Rose Schneiderman Papers, Tamiment Institute Library, New York University, New York.

30. Roosevelt endorsed female suffrage in 1912.

31. Ida Husted Harper, ed., *The History of Woman Suffrage* (New York, 1922), vol. 5, 165–66.

32. Nancy Cott, *The Grounding of Modern Feminism* (New Haven, Conn., 1987).

33. Ellen DuBois, "Working Women, Class Relations, and Suffrage Militance: Harriet Stanton Blatch and the New York Suffrage Movement, 1894–1909," *Journal of American History* 74 (June 1987), 41–42. Also, Nancy Cott observes that "an important inspiration for privileged women's political activism in this period . . . was their sense that wage-earners . . . were exemplars of independent womanhood." Cott, *The Grounding of Modern Feminism*, 33.

34. Carroll Smith-Rosenberg, *Disorderly Conduct: Visions of Gender in Victorian America* (New York, 1985). Smith-Rosenberg, although not writing specifically of suffragists, claims that "the second generation of New Women fused their challenge of gender conventions with a repudiation of bourgeois sexual norms" (177). When writing of the 1880s, she declares, "The new bourgeois order, supported by its professional cohorts, could now endow its expressive vocabulary with political and bureaucratic power" (180). On the "new woman," see also Elaine Showalter, *Sexual Anarchy: Gender and Culture in the Fin de Siècle* (New York, 1990).

35. In writing of the Equality League for Self-Supporting Women of which Barnum was a member, DuBois claims that their militant style of suffrage activ-

ism was influenced by trade unionism. DuBois, "Working-Class Women, Class Relations," 42.

36. DuBois contends that the term "middle class" creates confusion when used with reference to this small emergent group, which was distinguished by a historically unique configuration of education, income, and status. DuBois, "Working Class Women, Class Relations."

37. Gertrude Barnum to Samuel Gompers, 5 October 1917, Annie Keeney O'Sullivan Papers, Arthur and Elizabeth Schlesinger Library, Radcliffe College, Cambridge, Mass.

38. *Boston Globe*, 29 October 1917. The reception was hosted by Mrs. Frederick Bagley, chairwoman of the Americanization committee of the National Woman Suffrage Association. Also see John F. McClymer, "Women as Americanizers, and as Americanized," unpublished paper.

39. Pauline Newman, "Women and Work," *Ladies' Garment Worker* 3 (December 1916): 22, 26.

40. Aileen Kraditor, *The Ideas of the Woman Suffrage Movement, 1890–1920* (New York, 1971); Eleanor Flexner, *Century of Struggle: The Woman's Rights Movement in the United States* (New York, 1974); Susan Englander, "Organizing for Woman Suffrage in 'Labor's City': The Wage Earner's League's Unique Role in the 1911 Campaign in San Francisco," unpublished paper, San Francisco, 1986; Ronald Schaffer, "The Problem of Consciousness in the Woman Suffrage Movement: A California Perspective," *Pacific Historical Review* 45 (November 1976): 469–93; Sharon Hartman Strom, "Leadership and Tactics in the American Woman Suffrage Movement: A New Perspective from Massachusetts," *Journal of American History* (September 1975); Elinor Lerner, "Immigrant and Working Class Involvement in the New York City Woman Suffrage Movement, 1905–1917: A Study in Progressive Era Politics" (Ph.D. diss., University of California, Berkeley, 1981).

41. Elinor Lerner, "Immigrant and Working Class."

42. James Kloppenberg, *Uncertain Victory: Social Democracy and Progressivism in European and American Thought, 1870–1920* (New York, 1986). Kloppenberg argues that the theory of social democracy emerged in the 1890s from "Marxist and utopian socialism and from the tradition of Christian social criticism . . . from German and English economic theory, classical positivism, and Darwinian evolutionary theory" (5–6).

43. Albert Gallatin, secretary of the treasury under Jefferson and Madison, first developed the concept of industrial democracy.

44. The Webbs are quoted in Milton Derber, *The American Idea of Industrial Democracy, 1865–1965* (Urbana, Ill., 1970). Derber notes that the Webbs also defined industrial democracy as simply the "institution of trade unionism per se" (10). Steven Fraser also discusses industrial democracy, in *Labor Will Rule: Sidney Hillman and the Rise of American Labor* (New York, 1991).

45. "Mrs. [*sic*] Barnum Interviews Morris Black," *Ladies' Garment Worker* (n.d.): 5ff.

46. Barnum recommended, for example, that consumers cast "the industrial ballot of their purchasing power for garments made in protocol factories." Gertrude Barnum, "How Industrial Peace Has Been Brought About in the Clothing Trade," *Independent* (3 October 1912): 777, 778, 780.

47. Gertrude Barnum, "The Living Skeleton and the Stout Reformer," *Ladies' Garment Worker* 1 (July 1910): 3.

48. Gertrude Barnum, "How Industrial Peace," 779.

49. According to Barnum, the protocol provided for a " 'preferential' shop [not a closed shop], union hours and prices, lower and higher 'courts' for the adjudication of industrial disputes, and a joint board of sanitary control." Barnum, "How Industrial Peace," 777.

50. Gertrude Barnum, "How Industrial Peace," and "First Fruits of the Protocol," *Independent* (3 October 1912): 74–75.

51. Melvyn Dubofsky, *Industrialism and the American Worker, 1865–1920* (New York, 1975), and *When Workers Organize* (Amherst, Mass., 1968).

52. Gertrude Barnum, untitled draft of article, Annie Keeney O'Sullivan Papers, Arthur and Elizabeth Schlesinger Library, Radcliffe College.

53. Melvyn Dubofsky, "Gertrude Barnum," in *Notable American Women*, vol. 1, ed. Edward T. James et al. (Cambridge, Mass., 1981), 93–94.

54. Paula Baker, "The Domestication of Politics," 644.

55. Nancy Schrom Dye characterized Barnum's early stories as illustrating the WTUL's trade union philosophy. *As Equals and As Sisters*, 69.

56. Gertrude Barnum, "The Idealists," *Ladies' Garment Worker* (April 1912). Six of Barnum's published short stories are reprinted in *Sealskin and Shoddy: Working Women in American Labor Press Fiction, 1870–1920*, ed. Ann Schofield (Westport, Conn., 1988), 153–64.

57. Gertrude Barnum, "The Long Faced Girl," manuscript, Annie Keeney O'Sullivan Papers, Arthur and Elizabeth Schlesinger Library, Radcliffe College. n.p.

58. Gertrude Barnum, "Her Sister's Leavings," manuscript, Annie Keeney O'Sullivan Papers, Arthur and Elizabeth Schlesinger Library, Radcliffe College.

59. Gertrude Barnum, "In the Jacket Shop: A Story," *Ladies' Garment Worker* 5 (June 1912): 5.

60. Gertrude Barnum, untitled story, Annie Keeney O'Sullivan Papers, Arthur and Elizabeth Schlesinger Library, Radcliffe College.

61. Gertrude Barnum, "Fortune Tellers," story, Annie Keeney O'Sullivan Papers, Arthur and Elizabeth Schlesinger Library, Radcliffe College.

62. Gertrude Barnum, "Shuttleville Strike," story (unpaginated), Annie Keeney O'Sullivan Papers, Arthur and Elizabeth Schlesinger Library, Radcliffe College.

63. Michael Denning, *Mechanic Accents: The Dime Novel and Working Class Culture* (London, 1987), 78.

64. "Gertrude Barnum Talks to Girls," *New York World*, 6 June 1907, n.p.

65. Gertrude Barnum, "The Third Sex in Industry," *New York Times Maga-zine* (30 March 1919): 7–10.

66. Michael Denning, *Mechanic Accents*, 81.

67. Gertrude Barnum, "The Pig-Headed Girl," *Ladies' Garment Worker* 3 (April 1912): 26–27; see also Ann Schofield, ed., *Sealskin and Shoddy*; and Ann Schofield, "From 'Sealskin and Shoddy' to 'The Pig-Headed Girl': Patriarchal Fable for Workers," in *"To Toil the Livelong Day": America's Women at Work, 1780–1980*, ed. Carol Groneman and Mary Beth Norton (Ithaca, N.Y., 1987), 112–24.

68. Gertrude Barnum, "The Perfect Lady," *New York World*, n.d.

69. Mary V. Dearborn, *Pocahontas's Daughters: Gender and Ethnicity in American Culture* (New York, 1986); Hasia Diner, *Erin's Daughters in America: Irish Immigrant Women in the Nineteenth Century* (Baltimore, 1983).

2. MARY DREIER / 1876–1963

1. *Survey*, 3 November 1909.

2. *American Journal Examiner*, 1 November 1909.

3. Agnes Nestor, *Woman's Labor Leader: An Autobiography of Agnes Nestor* (Rockford, Ill., 1954), 108. Mary Elizabeth Dreier (hereafter cited as MED) to manager, Ladies' Whitegood Workers, 22 August 1959, quoted in Elizabeth Anne Payne, *Reform, Labor, and Feminism: Margaret Dreier Robins and the Women's Trade Union League* (Urbana, Ill., 1988), 137.

4. Mary Goff to MED, 4 December 1929, Mary Elizabeth Dreier Papers, Arthur and Elizabeth Schlesinger Library, Radcliffe College, Cambridge, Mass. (hereafter cited as MED Papers).

5. Elizabeth Payne Moore, "Mary Elizabeth Dreier," in *Notable American Women: The Modern Era*, ed. Edward T. James (Cambridge, Mass., 1971), 205.

6. "The Reminiscences of Frances Perkins" (1955), Oral History Collection, Columbia University, New York, 139, 140, 141, 142.

7. Ellen Condliffe Lagemann, *A Generation of Women: Education in the Lives of Progressive Reformers* (Cambridge, Mass., 1979), 129.

8. Kathryn Kish Sklar, "The Historical Foundations of Women's Power in the Creation of the American Welfare State," in *Mothers of a New World: Mater-nalist Politics and the Origins of Welfare States*, ed. Seth Koven and Sonya Michel (New York, 1993), 51. Sklar notes the "most massive features" of this group after 1900 were "its massive grass-roots scale and its institutional auton-omy" (ibid.).

9. Mary E. Dreier, *Margaret Dreier Robins: Her Life, Letters, and Work* (New York, 1950). The Dreier tradition of charitable work extended back to seventeenth-century Germany.

10. Ibid., 9–11.

11. Payne, *Reform, Labor*, 13.

12. Mary E. Dreier, "Barbara Richards" (1914), manuscript, MED Papers.

13. Ibid., 10.

14. Ibid., 12.

15. Ibid., 157.

16. MED, undelivered speech to Women's City Club (1933), MED Papers.

17. Denning points out that working girls are almost always presented as orphans in factory girl melodramas. Michael Denning, *Mechanic Accents: The Dime Novel and Working Class Culture* (London, 1987).

18. MED, "Barbara Richards," 234.

19. Ibid., 158.

20. MED to Leonora O'Reilly, 19 June 1908, quoted in Nancy Schrom Dye, *As Equals and as Sisters: Feminism, Unionism, and the Women's Trade Union League of New York* (Columbia, Mo., 1980), 56.

21. Dye, *As Equals and as Sisters*, 56.

22. Payne, *Reform, Labor*, 34.

23. I am indebted to Elizabeth Anne Payne for this anecdote.

24. Frances Kellor to MED, 3 November 1906, MED Papers.

25. Frances Kellor to MED, 5 December 1904, MED Papers.

26. Frances Kellor to MED, 12 December 1905, MED Papers.

27. Margaret Dreier Robins to MED, 5 June 1905, MED Papers. See Susan Ware, *Partner and I: Molly Dewson, Feminism, and New Deal Politics* (New Haven, Conn., 1987), 57ff., for a list of such "marriages" and a discussion of their social meaning.

28. Payne, *Reform, Labor*, 32.

29. MED, "To Trade Union Women," *Life and Labor* 3 (February 1913): n.p. Hasia Diner and other historians of immigration claim, contrary to Dreier's beliefs, that many young immigrant women were attracted to the United States not by abstract ideals of freedom but rather by the opportunity to make a good marriage. Hasia R. Diner, *Erin's Daughters in America: Irish Immigrant Women in the Nineteenth Century* (Baltimore, 1983).

30. MED, "Lines," *Life and Labor* 3 (June 1913): 191. This poem was directed to Boston readers, who, she wrote, "Will stand by fragile women and young girls / Whose vision is the new democracy."

31. MED, "The Neckwear Workers and Their Strike," *Life and Labor* 3 (December 1913): 356–58.

32. Two excellent histories of the WTUL are Nancy S. Dye, *As Equals and as Sisters*, and Elizabeth Anne Payne, *Reform, Labor*.

33. David Montgomery, *The Fall of the House of Labor: The Workplace, the State, and American Labor Activism, 1865–1925* (Cambridge, 1987); Melvyn Dubofsky, *Industrialism and the American Worker, 1865–1920* (Arlington Heights, Ill., 1985). David Brody, *In Labor's Cause: Main Themes in the History of the American Worker* (New York, 1993).

34. Untitled essay, n.d., MED Papers.

35. MED, "Expansion Through Agitation and Education," *Life and Labor* 11 (June 1921): 163–65, 192.

36. Dreier's pragmatic approach would put her in the category "social feminist," although Nancy Cott has recently and effectively criticized the use of that term. On social feminism, see William L. O'Neill, *Everyone Was Brave: A History of Feminism in America* (Chicago, 1969), and J. Stanley Lemons, *The Woman Citizen: Social Feminism in the 1920s* (Urbana, Ill., 1973). See also Nancy F. Cott, *The Grounding of Modern Feminism* (New Haven, Conn., 1987), and Cott, "What's in a Name: The Limits of 'Social Feminism'; or, Expanding the Vocabulary of Women's History," *Journal of American History* 76 (December 1989): 809–29.

37. George Martin, *Madame Secretary: Frances Perkins* (Boston, 1976), 88. Leon Stein, *The Triangle Fire* (Philadelphia, 1962), 147–57.

38. Other members of the commission included state senator Robert Wagner (chair), assemblyman Al Smith (vice chair), Charles Hamilton, Edward Jackson, Cyrus W. Phillips, and, as public members, Simon Brentano, publisher and bookseller, Robert E. Dowling, realtor, and Samuel Gompers, AFL president.

39. Martin, *Madame Secretary*, 89, 104.

40. Martin, *Madame Secretary*, 112.

41. Martin, *Madame Secretary*, 89, 104, 112.

42. For an excellent description of the New York Women's City Club, see Elisabeth Israels Perry, *Belle Moskowitz: Feminine Politics and the Exercise of Power in the Age of Alfred E. Smith* (New York, 1987), 112–13, 145ff. Moskowitz, Al Smith's political strategist and campaign manager, frequently sought support for Smith's programs at the Women's City Club. Following passage of the suffrage amendment, membership in the club soared to 3,000.

43. MED to Leonora O'Reilly, 16 September 1916. Quoted in Nancy Schrom Dye, *As Equals and as Sisters*, 122; Mary J. Bularzik, "The Bonds of Belonging: Leonora O'Reilly and Social Reform," *Labor Hisotry* 24 (Winter 1983): 76–77.

44. Frances Perkins, who was closely associated with the commission, found that the experience "caused her to develop a lifelong conviction that the best way to improve conditions for workers was through legislation not unions." Martin, *Madame Secretary*, 120.

45. See Dye, *As Equals and as Sisters*, chap. 6, for a discussion of the WTUL and suffrage.

46. Dye, *As Equals and as Sisters*, 122.

47. Dye, *As Equals and as Sisters*, 139.

48. The work of the Equality League is discussed in Ellen Carol DuBois, "Working Women, Class Relations, and Suffrage Militance: Harriet Stanton Blatch and the New York Woman Suffrage Movement, 1894–1909," *Journal of American History* 74 (June 1987), 34–58, and Cott, *The Grounding of Modern Feminism*, 25.

49. Dye, *As Equals and as Sisters*, 130.

50. The referendum lost in the state by 200,000 votes and in New York City by 89,000 votes. Dye, *As Equals and as Sisters*, 136.

51. On the suffrage campaign in New York, also see Ronald Schaeffer, "The New York City Woman Suffrage Party, 1909–1919," *New York History* 43 (July 1962): 268–87; Elinor Lerner, "Immigrant and Working Class Involvement in the New York City Women's Suffrage Movement, 1905–1917: A Study in Progressive Era Politics" (Ph.D. diss., University of California, Berkeley, 1981).

52. DuBois, "Working Women, Class Relations," 43.

53. The groups that composed the conference were the New York State and City Consumer's League, the YWCA, the New York State Women's Suffrage Party, and the New York Women's Trade Union League. They supported legislation for the eight-hour day, a minimum wage, health insurance, and protection for office workers, transportation workers, and elevator operators. Perry, *Belle Moskowitz*, 144. Marion Dickerman, eulogy for MED, Marion Dickerman Papers, Franklin D. Roosevelt Library, Hyde Park, New York. Hereafter cited as MD Papers. "The Reminiscences of Marion Dickerman" (1973), 369–73, Oral History Collection, Columbia University, New York.

54. Dickerman, eulogy, 4.

55. Dickerman, eulogy, 5.

56. Dickerman and her partner, Nancy Cook, remained close to Mary Dreier throughout her life. In 1922 and 1923, Dickerman taught English at the Bryn Mawr Summer School for Women Workers and invited Dreier to Philadelphia to share her experiences, particularly of the FIC with the worker-students. Following Dreier's death, Dickerman delivered a eulogy that spoke of politics, reform, and, of course, Dreier's beauty.

57. Susan Ware, *Partner and I*.

58. Ibid., 33.

59. MED, "Some Industrial Conditions in Belgium," *Life and Labor* 9 (October 1919): 254–56.

60. MED, "Karl Legien," *Life and Labor* 9 (September 1919): 283–85.

61. MED, *Margaret Dreier Robins*, 139ff., 157ff. In the 1950s and early 1960s, in correspondence with Norman Cousins and Scott Nearing, Dreier reflected an avid interest in the situation of farmers, events in China, and nuclear questions. She subscribed to the newsletters of radicals I. F. Stone and Anna Louise Strong.

62. MED to Miss Louise L. Fernald, 1926 (?), Raymond Robins Papers, State Historical Society of Wisconsin, Madison.

63. Elisabeth Israels Perry, "Training for Public Life: ER and Women's Political Networks in the 1920s," in *Without Precedent: The Life and Career of Eleanor Roosevelt*, ed. Joan Hoff-Wilson and Marjorie Lightman (Bloomington, Ind., 1984), 28–45.

64. Paula Baker, "The Domestication of Politics: Women and American Political Society, 1780–1920," *American Historical Review* 89 (June 1984): 640.

65. MED, *Margaret Dreier Robins*, 174–75.

66. Dreier's other depression-era activities included: membership in the Regional Labor Board of New York, the Minimum Wage Board for Hotel and Restaurant Industry (she was labor representative), the Advisory Council of the U.S. and New York State Employment Services, and the General Advisory Board on the New York Minimum Wage.

67. MED to Hon. Henry F. Ashurst, 27 February 1938, MED Papers.

68. MED, "Radio Talk for the American Labor Party," 15 October 1937, MED Papers.

69. MED to Frieda Miller, 17 July 1938, MED Papers.

70. Pauline Newman to MED, 9 February 1949, MED Papers.

71. A 1940 memo indicated that WTUL members were represented in the Inter-American Commission of Women, the Associated Farm Women of America, the American Academy of Political and Social Science, the National YWCA, the American Association for Labor Legislation, the American Home Economics Association, and the Civil Liberties Conference.

72. On the history of the ERA struggle, see Leila Rupp and Verta Taylor, *Survival in the Doldrums: The American Women's Rights Movement, 1945 to the 1960s* (New York, 1987); Cynthia Harrison, *On Account of Sex: The Politics of Women's Issues, 1945–1968* (Berkeley, 1988); Judith Sealander, *As Minority Becomes Majority; Federal Reaction to the Phenomenon of Women in the Workforce, 1920–1963* (Westport, Conn., 1983); Judith Baer, *The Chains of Protection: Judicial Response to Women's Labor Legislation* (Westport, Conn., 1978); Susan Becker, *The Origins of the Equal Rights Amendment: American Feminism Between the Wars* (Westport, Conn., 1981).

73. Elisabeth Christman to Executive Board, WTUL, 3 August 1944, MED Papers. Some organizations that joined with the WTUL in opposition to the ERA were: the National League of Women Voters, the YWCA, the Consumer's League, the National Council of Jewish Women, the American Association of University Women, the National Catholic Welfare Conference.

74. MED to Elisabeth Christman, 26 January 1944, MED Papers.

75. Ibid.

76. In 1949 Rose Schneiderman retired after thirty years as president of the New York League, saying, "The progress we made was beyond our wildest dreams" and "I'm tired. It's time the younger members took over the league's work" (*New York Times*, 7 April 1949).

77. Pauline Newman to MED, 15 February 1951, MED Papers.

78. *New York Times*, 15 June 1950, p. 7.

79. MED to Rose Schneiderman, 30 July 1962, MED Papers.

3. PAULINE NEWMAN / C. 1888–1986

1. Pauline M. Newman, interview by Barbara Wertheimer, New York, N.Y., November 1976, transcript in Pauline M. Newman Papers, Arthur and Elizabeth Schlesinger Library, Radcliffe College, Cambridge, Mass. (hereafter cited as PMN Papers).

2. Pauline Newman, "Friends Who Contribute to This Issue," *Life and Labor* 11 (June 1921): 161.

3. The Newman family Bible, which contained Pauline's birthdate, was lost on the voyage to America. She took 18 October as her birthday to commemorate the Russian Revolution.

4. Newman rarely mentioned her mother and regarded her father as the more influential parent. In one interview she spoke of her mother's life in America: "I don't know . . . how much she was concerned with things outside the house and sometimes I have a feeling that she was really quite lonely. . . . My mother took care; she did the shopping, prepared the meal. . . . she didn't have anything else to do." *Twentieth Century Trade Union Women: Vehicle for Social Change Oral History Project* (Sanford, N.C.: Microfilming Corporation of America, 1979).

5. Information on Newman's early life can be found in the previously cited interview by Barbara Wertheimer and also in interviews by Henoch Mendelsund for YIVO in 1973 and by Betty Yorburg for the Socialist Movements Collection, Columbia University, in 1965. Transcripts of these interviews are included in the PMN Papers. See also an edited interview with Newman in Joan Morrison and Charlotte Fox Zabusky, eds., *American Mosaic: The Immigrant Experience in the Words of Those Who Lived It* (New York, 1980). On women's lives in east European shtetls, see Sydney Stahl Weinberg, *World of Our Mothers* (Chapel Hill, N.C., 1988), and Susan A. Glenn, *Daughters of the Shtetl: Life and Labor in the Immigrant Generation* (Ithaca, N.Y., 1990).

6. PMN to Michael and Hugh Owen, 10 September 1952, PMN Papers.

7. PMN, interview by Barbara Wertheimer.

8. *Spokesman Review*, Spokane, Wash., n.d. (copy in PMN Papers).

9. PMN, interview by Barbara Wertheimer.

10. On the Uprising, see Melvyn Dubofsky, *When Workers Organize: New York City in the Progressive Era* (Amherst, Mass., 1968); Ann Schofield, "The Uprising of the 20,000: The Making of a Labor Legend," in *A Needle, A Bobbin, A Strike: Women Needleworkers in America*, ed. Joan Jensen and Sue Davidson (Philadelphia, 1984), 167–82; Meredith Tax, *The Rising of the Women: Feminist Solidarity and Class Conflict, 1880–1917* (New York, 1980).

11. PMN, "Lest We Forget," *Message*, March 1917, pp. 3–4.

12. See, for example, PMN, "Lest We Forget."

13. Lois Scharf, "The Great Uprising in Cleveland: When Sisterhood

Failed," in *A Needle, A Bobbin*, 146–66. For Newman's own account of the strike, which emphasizes its particularly violent nature, see "From the Battlefield," *Life and Labor* 1 (October 1911): 297.

14. Scharf, "The Great Uprising," 155.

15. Karen M. Mason, "Feeling the Pinch: The Kalamazoo Corsetmakers' Strike of 1912," in *"To Toil the Livelong Day": America's Women at Work, 1780–1980*, ed. Carol Groneman and Mary Beth Norton (Ithaca, N.Y., 1987), 141–60. Mason explains the complicated reasons why this strategy failed and suggests that the strike was really unwinnable by the time Newman arrived in June.

16. Mason, "Feeling the Pinch," 154.

17. *Kalamazoo Telegraph Press*, 5, 6, and 7 June 1912, quoted in Mason, "Feeling the Pinch," 154.

18. In an article about the needs of working girls in the *Detroit Times*, Newman flatly stated, "I realize that each of these, important as it may be, is subsidiary to the economic problem." Quoted in Mason, "Feeling the Pinch," 158.

19. Mason, "Feeling the Pinch"; Pauline Newman, "News from Kalamazoo," *Ladies' Garment Worker* 3 (December 1912): 3–4.

20. Benjamin Stolberg, *Tailor's Progress* (Garden City, N.Y., 1944), 42.

21. Roger Waldinger, "Another Look at the International Ladies' Garment Workers' Union: Women, Industry Structure, and Collective Action," in *Women, Work, and Protest: A Century of U.S. Women's Labor History*, ed. Ruth Milkman (Boston, 1985), 86–109; Alice Kessler-Harris, "Organizing the Unorganizable: Three Jewish Women and Their Union," *Labor History* 17 (Winter 1976): 14–28.

22. PMN to Rose Schneiderman, 13 September 1910, Rose Schneiderman Papers, Tamiment Institute, New York University, New York (hereafter cited as RS Papers).

23. PMN to Rose Schneiderman, 14 November 1911, RS Papers.

24. Pauline Newman, "Our Women Workers," *Ladies' Garment Worker* (May 1913): 18.

25. In "The Long Working Day and Spring," *Life and Labor* (May 1912): 135, she linked union membership to shorter hours to the chance to enjoy spring.

26. PMN, "The Women's Trade Union League in the New York Labor Day Parade," *Life and Labor* (November 1911): 326.

27. On these distinctions, see Nancy Cott, *The Grounding of Modern Feminism* (New Haven, Conn., 1987), and Rosalind Rosenberg, *Beyond Separate Spheres: Intellectual Roots of Modern Feminism* (New Haven, Conn., 1982).

28. Interview by Barbara Wertheimer, 49.

29. Mari Jo Buhle, *Women and American Socialism, 1870–1920* (Urbana, Ill., 1981), 240, 219.

30. PMN, "Woman Suffrage: A Means to an End," *New York Call* (2 May 1914): 4. Buhle claims that arguments about the social responsibility of mothers were "pioneered by the WCTU" (Women's Christian Temperance Union). Buhle, *Women and American Socialism*, 220.

31. For a discussion of these different tendencies, see Françoise Basch (trans. Nancy Festinger), "The Socialist Party of America, the Woman Question, and Theresa Serber Malkiel," in *Women in Culture and Politics: A Century of Change*, ed. Judith Friedlander et al. (Bloomington, Ind., 1986), 344–57.

32. Newman went on to urge her readers to take out their naturalization papers. PMN, "Are You Ready to Use Your New Power?" *Message* (n.d.). The Second International Directive "ordered socialist parties in all countries to support women's suffrage, but barred women from abandoning the socialist struggle for the salons of bourgeois suffragists." Basch, "The Socialist Party," 348. For a discussion of socialists and female suffrage, see Buhle, *Women and American Socialism*; Sally Miller, ed., *Flawed Liberation: Socialism and Feminism* (Westport, Conn., 1981).

33. PMN to Rose Schneiderman, 16 January 1912, RS Papers.

34. PMN to Rose Schneiderman, 21 November 1911, RS Papers.

35. PMN to Rose Schneiderman, 30 January 1912, RS Papers.

36. PMN, "Her Choice" (1912), PMN Papers.

37. Abraham Cahan, *The Rise of David Levinsky* (Gloucester, Mass., 1960); Alice Kessler-Harris, introduction to Anzia Yezierska, *The Breadgivers* (New York, 1975), ix. Other autobiographies of Jewish immigrant women include Rose Cohen, *Out of the Shadow* (New York, 1971); Lucy Robins Lang, *Tomorrow Is Beautiful* (New York, 1948); Emma Goldman, *Living My Life* (New York, 1931); Rose Pesotta, *Bread upon the Waters* (Ithaca, N.Y., 1987); Rose Schneiderman, *All for One* (New York, 1967).

38. Although Newman repudiated religious Judaism (even her mother wasn't observant after leaving Europe), her participation in the rich yeast of secular Jewish culture, with its cafes, literary societies, music, and theater, facilitated her passage into a more "modern" life.

39. PMN, interview by Barbara Wertheimer, 40.

40. Linda Gordon, "Social Insurance and Public Assistance: The Influence of Gender in Welfare Thought in the United States, 1890–1935," *American Historical Review* 97 (February 1992): 19–54; Alice Kessler-Harris, "Problems of Coalition-Building: Women and Trade Unions in the 1920s," in *Women, Work, and Protest: A Century of U.S. Women's Labor History*, ed. Ruth Milkman (Boston, 1985), 110–39; Ellen Carol DuBois, "Harriet Stanton Blatch and the Transformation of Class Relations Among Woman Suffragists," in *Gender, Class, Race, and Reform in the Progressive Era*, ed. Noralee Frankel and Nancy S. Dye (Lexington, Ky., 1991), 162–89.

41. Alice Kessler-Harris, "Rose Schneiderman and the Limits of Women's Trade Unionism," in *Labor Leaders in America*, ed. Melvyn Dubofsky and Warren Van Tine (Urbana, Ill., 1987), 161.

42. "Woman and Her Interests," *American Hebrew* (15 September 1916): 590.

43. PMN, interview by Henoch Mendelsund, cited in note five. Newman's continued affinity for the Left inspired Newman to write to her companion, Frieda Miller, in 1927: "Dear Girl, It is raining—and today it should. Sacco and Vanzetti have been officially murdered and there is no place for sunshine today." Her letter describes the protest against the anarchists' execution and Newman's anguish at their death. She concluded, "It is still raining and the heart is heavy while the spirit wanders toward you—where it might find some peace." PMN to Frieda Miller, 23 August 1927, Frieda Miller Papers, Arthur and Elizabeth Schlesinger Library, Radcliffe College, Cambridge, Mass.

44. In 1926, N.Y. League president Rose Schneiderman organized a conference on southern organizing, and between 1927 and 1931 the WTUL mounted an organizing campaign in the South.

45. Alice Kessler-Harris defines this dichotomy as "dual closure" between "exclusion" and "usurpation." Kessler-Harris, "Coalition-Building," 122.

46. PMN, interview by Barbara Wertheimer, 40.

47. Kessler-Harris, "Coalition-Building," 125.

48. "Just Notes," 3 April 1975, PMN Papers.

49. Interview by Henoch Mendelsund, December 1973. Biographical material on Frieda Miller can be found in *Notable American Women*. The Frieda Miller papers are at the Schlesinger Library. Miller's daughter, Elisabeth Burger, claimed that Miller represented an "ideal" for Newman: "blonde, well-educated, comfortable in society, admired." Elisabeth Burger, interview with author, 1988.

50. Blanche Wiesen Cook, " 'Women Alone Stir My Imagination': Lesbianism and the Cultural Tradition," *Signs* 4 (Summer 1979): 738. On women's relationships, see also Lillian Faderman, *Surpassing the Love of Men: Romantic Friendships and Love Between Women from the Renaissance to the Present* (New York, 1981); Carroll Smith-Rosenberg, "The Female World of Love and Ritual: Relationships Between Women in Nineteenth-Century America," *Signs* 1 (Autumn 1975): 27; *Frontiers* 4 (Fall 1979) (lesbian history issue).

51. Susan Ware comments on the relationship between Molly Dewson and Polly Porter: "In the end, of course, what is important is not what they did in bed, but that they chose each other, loved each other, and expressed that love through a lifetime of shared partnership." Susan Ware, *Partner and I: Molly Dewson, Feminism, and New Deal Politics* (New Haven, Conn., 1987), 59.

52. Elisabeth Burger, eulogy for PMN, International Ladies' Garment Workers' Archives, New York (now housed at the School of Labor and Industrial Relations, Cornell University, Ithaca, N.Y.).

53. Barbara Wertheimer, interview by author, 1983; Elisabeth Burger, interview by author, 1988. Newman, however, in a 1973 interview claimed that Miller had "adopted" a daughter.

54. Berger, eulogy.

55. Rosalind Rosenberg writes of the difficulty for women during this period of combining marriage and professional life; see *Beyond Separate Spheres: The Intellectual Roots of Modern Feminism* (New Haven, Conn., 1982).

56. Berger, eulogy.

57. Historians who discuss the concept and meaning of women's networks include: Mary P. Ryan, "The Power of Women's Networks: A Case Study of Female Moral Reform in Antebellum America," *Feminist Studies* 5 (Spring 1979): 66–85; Carroll Smith-Rosenberg, "The Female World"; Blanche Wiesen Cook, "Female Support Networks"; Linda Gordon, "Social Insurance and Public Assistance: The Influence of Gender in Welfare Thought in the United States, 1890–1935," *American Historical Review* 97 (February 1992): 19–54. My use of the concept "network" is most like Susan Ware's in *Beyond Suffrage: Women and the New Deal* (Cambridge, Mass., 1981).

58. Linda Gordon, "Social Insurance," 26. Of seventy-six female social reformers in her sample, Gordon found that 28 percent lived in "Boston marriages."

59. Irving Bernstein, *The Lean Years: A History of the American Worker, 1920–1933* (Baltimore, 1966), 85. The union's situation had worsened by the 1930s, Berstein notes. Its "very existence [was] threatened by the collapse of the International Madison Bank . . . The ILGWU was unable to meet payments on outstanding bonds and instituted a vigorous economic program. . . . President Benjamin Schlesinger begged New York's lieutenant governor Herbert Lehman for a loan of $10,000 which Lehman was unable to grant." Bernstein, 337.

60. PMN, interview by Barbara Wertheimer, 60.

61. *Industrial Bulletin* (17 June 1952): 1.

62. Diane Kirkby, "The Wage-Earning Woman and the State: The National Women's Trade Union League and Protective Labor Legislation, 1903–1923," *Labor History* 28 (Winter 1987): 54–74.

63. *Protective Legislation in Danger*, report of the Conference of Trade Union Women, 26 February 1922, PMN Papers.

64. Kessler-Harris, "Coalition-Building," 132.

65. Typescript, n.d., p. 3, PMN Papers.

66. Kirkby, "Wage-Earning Woman," 56.

67. Mary Gilson to PMN, 28 March 1938, PMN Papers. Gilson wrote to Newman to commend her for the "great impression" she had made before the Senate Committee on Equal Rights.

68. Joseph Lash, *Eleanor and Franklin: The Story of Their Relationship, Based on Eleanor Roosevelt's Private Papers* (New York, 1971), 438–39. Rose Schneiderman with Lucy Goldthwaite, *All for One* (New York, 1967), 175–76.

69. PMN, interview by Betty Yorburg.

70. The American Labor Party was founded by ILGWU president David

Dubinsky to circumvent conservative Democrats of New York's Tammany Hall. It mobilized labor votes for FDR.

71. See, for example, her article "First Minimum Wage Law Goes into Effect," written for *American Labor World* 5 (November 1933): 17. In 1922 she was on the advisory editorial board of *Labor Age*, whose board of directors included such prominent leftists as Elizabeth Gurley Flynn and whose masthead bore the slogan "Believing that the goal of the American labor movement lies in the socialization of industry."

72. PMN, "The Job Ahead—For All of Us," n.d., PMN Papers.

73. PMN, "Labor's Unfinished Business," *Jewish Daily Forward*, n.d., draft in PMN Papers. Newman's sense of labor's progress was even more vividly expressed on Labor Day, 1956. She recalled reading the "labor poets" early in the century and remarked, "Oh, if only those men who wrote those poems could see labor today! Labor grown up, mature, experienced, informed and intelligent. Labor alert, articulate and determined to be no one's slave." "Labor Day Greetings," n.d., PMN Papers.

74. PMN traveled to Latin America under the auspices of the League (in 1936 to Guatemala and in 1941 to Equador). See "A Shirt Factory in Guatemala City," n.d., PMN Papers. Newman's work with the United Nations ILO has been noted in the text. She also served as a representative of the International Confederation of Free Trade Unions to the United Nations Commission on the Status of Women in the 1950s.

75. Leon Edel, "The Figure Under the Carpet," in *Telling Lives*, ed. Marc Pachter (Philadelphia, 1981), 25.

76. Virginia Yans-McLaughlin, "Metaphors of Self in History: Subjectivity, Oral Narrative, and Immigration Studies," in *Immigration Reconsidered: History, Sociology and Politics*, ed. Virginia Yans-McLaughlin (New York, 1990), 254–92.

77. Elisabeth Burger, interview by the author. Also see Annelise Orleck, *Common Sense and a Little Fire: Women and Working Class Politics in the United States, 1900–1965*, (Chapel Hill, N.C., 1995).

78. PMN daybooks, 26 November 1970, 5 December 1970, PMN Papers.

4. ROSE PESOTTA / 1896–1965

1. One essay describes Masya Peisoty as "an intellectual and cultural leader of the town's Jewish community." *Biographical Directory of Labor* (Westport, Conn., 1974), 459.

2. Rose Pesotta with John Nicholas Beffel, "Smashing a Matzoth Trust in the Pale," Rose Pesotta Papers, New York Public Library, Rare Books and Manuscripts Division, Astor, Lenox, and Tilden Foundations, New York (hereafter cited as RP Papers).

3. Rose Pesotta, *Days of Our Lives* (Boston, 1958), 93.

4. RP speech, Los Angeles, 27 February 1942, RP Papers.

5. Dana Frank, "Housewives, Socialists, and the Politics of Food: The 1917 New York Cost-of-Living Protests," *Feminist Studies* 11 (1985): 255–85; Paula E. Hyman, "Immigrant Women and Consumer Protest: The New York City Kosher Meat Boycott of 1902," *American Jewish History* 70 (1980): 91–105.

6. RP diary, 22 July 1934, RP Papers.

7. Pesotta, *Days,* 218.

8. Rose Pesotta, *Bread upon the Waters* (New York, 1944), 9.

9. Ann Schofield, "The Uprising of the 20,000: The Making of a Union Legend," in *A Needle, A Bobbin, A Strike: Women Needleworkers in America,* ed. Joan Jensen and Sue Davidson (Philadelphia, 1984), 167–82.

10. Descriptions of anarchist culture can be found in Paul Avrich, *The Modern School Movement: Anarchism and Education in the United States* (Princeton, N.J., 1980), *Anarchist Portraits* (Princeton, N.J., 1988), and *Anarchist Voices* (Princeton, N.J., 1995). Paul Buhle writes of the "fundamental role" that anarchists played in "launching a modern labor movement among key groups" in the United States. He continues, "Without them craft and industrial unionism might not have happened for another generation. Certainly it would have lacked the verve, the dynamic impulse toward universality, the poetic spirit they imparted" (21). "Anarchism and American Labor," *International Labor and Working Class History* 23 (Spring 1983): 21–34.

11. Pesotta's activity in later life in such groups as the League for Industrial Democracy and the Workers' Defense Fund has led Gerald Sorin to term her a social democrat. Pesotta always identified herself, however, as an anarchist. Gerald Sorin, *Prophetic Minority* (Bloomington, Ind., 1985).

12. RP, "The Libertarian Program of Social Change," n.d., RP Papers, 2.

13. Pesotta's membership in "Friends of Emma Goldman" put her in the company of such prominent progressive figures as John Dewey, Freda Kirchwey, Norman Thomas, and Roger Baldwin.

14. Interview with Esther R. Leibowitz, 7 October 1983, quoted in Elaine Leeder, *The Gentle General: Rose Pesotta, Anarchist and Labor Organizer* (Albany, N.Y., 1993).

15. Bonnie Haaland, *Emma Goldman: Sexuality and the Impurity of the State* (Montreal, 1993).

16. RP to "A New Yorker," 18 January 1934, RP Papers. The anonymous critic may have been Mrs. Paul Berg.

17. Paul Avrich, *The Modern School Movement,* 280; *The Road to Freedom* (Westport, Conn., 1970), 2v. Paul Buhle comments, "In *Road,* as elsewhere in America, anarchism was an intensely ethical movement." Paul Buhle, "Introduction," *The Road to Freedom. The Road to Freedom* had about 3,000 subscribers. Avrich, *Anarchist Voices,* 432.

18. Rose Pesotta, "Road to Freedom Camp," *Road to Freedom* 2:11 (1

August 1926): 8, and "Boston, August 28, 1927," *Road to Freedom* 6:12 (August 1930): 1.

19. "Woman and the Fundamentalists," *Road to Freedom* 1:9 (July 1925): 1. This lengthy article argues that Christianity throughout the ages has portrayed women negatively. It concludes, "Woman demands and *commands* the rights over her own body" (ibid.).

20. RP Papers, box 25. Throughout her life Pesotta spoke frequently at rallies and meetings commemorating the anarchist martyrs. Jeannette Marks, *Thirteen Days* (New York, 1929), 59. Recalling Sacco and Vanzetti's funeral, Marks notes, "Toward the close of the march the struggles of the cortege with the police became more acute. But under the leadership of Rose Pesotta and Alfred Baker Lewis the sympathizers kept on, the police making last brutal efforts to incite them to violence" (ibid.).

21. Leeder, *The Gentle General*, 44.

22. RP to Hippolyte Havel, 10 February 1934; RP to Ann Winocu, 8 November 1934; RP Papers.

23. RP to Emil Olay, 10 September 1934, RP Papers. Pesotta was certainly not the only anarchist trade unionist. Paul Avrich notes a morally pragmatic approach by anarchist trade unionists: "They no longer disdained partial economic gains as many had done in the past." *Portraits*, 189–90.

24. Special correspondence, n.d., RP Papers.

25. Paul Avrich writes that Rose Pesotta, Morris Sigman, and Anna Sosnovsky became "enmeshed in the union hierarchy" as they battled to get communists out of the union. *Portraits*, 196. This anarchist faction in the ILGWU was cohesive enough to publish *Yunyon Arbeter*, a Yiddish newspaper. Avrich, *Anarchist Voices*, 350.

26. Rita Heller, "Blue Collars and Bluestockings: The Bryn Mawr Summer School for Workers," in *Sisterhood and Solidarity: Workers' Education for Women, 1914–1984*, ed. Joyce L. Kornbluh and Mary Frederickson (Philadelphia, 1984): 107–45; film "Women of Summer," Filmaker's Library, New York, 1985.

27. Heller, "Blue Collars," 118.

28. Pesotta, *Bread*, 15–16.

29. RP to "dearest comrade," 4 August 1922, RP Papers.

30. Len De Caux, *Labor Radical: From the Wobblies to the CIO* (Boston, 1970), 95–96.

31. Richard J. Altenbaugh, *Education for Struggle: The American Labor Colleges of the 1920s and 1930s* (Philadelphia, 1990); Charles F. Howlett, "Brookwood Labor College and Worker Commitment to Social Reform," *Mid-America* 61 (January 1979): 47–66. Richard J. Altenbaugh comments on the leadership of Brookside alumni like Pesotta, Len De Caux, Frank Winn, and the Reuther brothers at the famous Flint sit-down strike in 1936–37. He writes, "What unfolded at Flint assumed all of the characteristics of a textbook

version of a strike as taught at the labor colleges," 256. See also Steven Fraser, *Labor Will Rule: Sidney Hillman and the Rise of American Labor* (New York, 1991), 332.

32. Pesotta continued to support Brookwood. In 1936 she was invited to be a graduation speaker but had to decline. RP to Powers Hapgood, 27 March 1936, RP Papers.

33. RP to Mollie Steimer, 23 March 1925, Archives of the International Institute of Social History, Amsterdam, the Netherlands.

34. When A. J. Muste, the dean of Brookwood, visited rubber workers striking in Akron in 1936, Pesotta acknowledged his "practical and ethical" teaching. *Bread*, 225.

35. When American radio stations refused to allow the union airtime, Pesotta arranged to have strike news broadcast from a Tijuana station. *Bread*, 43.

36. Pesotta, *Bread*, chaps. 2, 3, 4, 5 (quotation on p. 63).

37. Pesotta, *Bread*, chaps. 6, 7, 8.

38. Pesotta, *Bread*, 101.

39. Pesotta, *Bread*, 158.

40. Susan A. Glenn, *Daughters of the Shtetl: Life and Labor in the Immigrant Generation* (Ithaca, N.Y., 1990), 217. On "new unionism," see also Steve Fraser, "The 'New Unionism' and the 'New Economic Policy,' " in *Work, Community, and Power: The Experience of Labor in Europe and America, 1900–1925*, ed. James E. Cronin and Carmen Sirianni (Philadelphia, 1983), 173–96, and J. M. Budish and George Soule, *The New Unionism in the Clothing Industry* (New York, 1920).

41. In San Francisco in 1933, she organized classes in "workers' problems and elementary economics, with emphasis on NRA Codes, union agreements and policies, and the reviewing of current literature on labor." Pesotta, *Bread*, 78.

42. Pesotta, *Bread*, 136, 228.

43. Pesotta, *Bread*, 198.

44. Pesotta, *Bread*, 159.

45. Pesotta, *Bread*, 170.

46. "The care with which I arranged for feeding the strikers had a definite purpose behind it. I wanted it known that the ILGWU provided well for its members involved in a dispute." Pesotta, *Bread*, 260.

47. Pesotta, *Bread*, 319.

48. Pesotta discovered that movies could be a "potent factor" in strikes and an effective vehicle in building a union culture.

49. Powers Hapgood to RP, 22 August 1941, RP Papers.

50. Susan A. Glenn, *Daughters of the Shtetl*, 6. Glenn comments, "It was this orientation toward partnership that gave Jewish women's activism its distinctive cast and its strongest contrast to the woman centered politics of American middle-class reformers" (ibid.).

51. Rose Pesotta, "In the Shop" (n.d.), RP Papers. See also "Shop Talk" and "Rudolph Valentino's Funeral," RP Papers.

52. RP to Israel Feinberg, 25 February 1934, RP Papers.

53. Pesotta, *Bread*, 332.

54. Pesotta, *Bread*, 337.

55. Pesotta, *Bread*, 337.

56. Pesotta, *Bread*, 392.

57. Rose Pesotta, "Report to the General Executive Board of the ILGWU," 15 June 1942, reprinted in John Laslett and Mary Tyler, *The ILGWU in Los Angeles, 1907–1988* (Los Angeles, 1989), 135–36. Monique Bourque provides a thorough and insightful analysis of Pesotta's activities in Los Angeles in " 'Toward a More Humane and Abundant Life': The Work of Anarchist Rose Pesotta in the ILGWU" (master's thesis, University of Delaware, c. 1992).

58. RP diary, 28 November 1944, RP Papers.

59. RP diary, 24 August 1948, RP Papers.

60. Rose Pesotta, "Statement" (address at the twenty-fifth annual meeting of the International Ladies' Garment Workers' Union, Boston, June 1944), 1–2 (copy in RP Papers).

61. Alice Kessler-Harris, "Organizing the Unorganizable: Three Jewish Women and Their Union," *Labor History* 17 (Winter 1976), 5–23.

62. Alice Kessler-Harris claims that Pesotta never married, while Elaine Leeder finds "documentation for only one legal marriage," although Pesotta claims in her memoirs that she married twice. The first "marriage" may have been to Israel Kasvan, with whom she lived for a few years in the 1920s. She was legally married in 1953 to Albert Martin (a.k.a. Frank Lopez), and they divorced several years later. During her years with the *Road to Freedom*, she is said to have had a relationship with Mateo Rico, a Sicilian active in the anarchist Spanish Cultura Proletarian Group. See Avrich, *Anarchist Voices*. Other men with whom Pesotta is known to have been involved include Kushnirov, Horst Borenz, and possibly Paul Berg.

63. Far fewer of Pesotta's letters to Hapgood exist, but enough remain to give the tone of the correspondence.

64. William Hapgood as quoted in Michael D. Marcaccio, *The Hapgoods: Three Earnest Brothers* (Charlottesville, Va., 1977), 209.

65. Powers Hapgood to Eleanor Hapgood and William Powers Hapgood, 27 January 1918, quoted in ibid., 218. On Powers Hapgood, see also Len De Caux, *Labor Radical: From the Wobblies to the CIO* (Boston, 1970), and Melvyn Dubofsky and Warren Van Tine, *John L. Lewis: A Biography* (New York, 1977).

66. Powers Hapgood to Rose Pesotta, 16 February 1943.

67. Donovan was the daughter of Irish immigrants and a graduate of the University of Michigan. She was a labor activist herself and, during the 1930s, worked for the Textile Workers' Organizing Committee. She and Hapgood had

two children, Barta and Donny. 1 March 1944, Powers Hapgood to John Beffel, RP Papers.

68. RP to Mary Donovan, 22 September 1936, RP Papers.

69. Powers Hapgood to RP, 26 August 1936, RP Papers.

70. Powers Hapgood to RP, 24 September 1936, RP Papers.

71. RP to Powers Hapgood, 26 September 1936, RP Papers.

72. RP to Powers Hapgood, 26 October 1936, RP Papers.

73. RP to Powers Hapgood, 18 July 1938, RP Papers.

74. RP to Powers Hapgood, 22 November 1944, RP Papers.

75. Powers Hapgood to RP, July 1937, RP Papers.

76. RP to Powers Hapgood, 30 January 1943, RP Papers.

77. RP, "Powers Hapgood—A Tribute," 8 February 1949, RP Papers.

78. RP diary, 5 February, 7 February 1949, RP Papers.

79. Powers Hapgood to RP, 26 September 1939, RP Papers. Pesotta also wrote an unpublished short story, "To a Spinster" (n.d.), that was addressed to a childless woman sitting on a park bench. She contrasts her unhappy lot with the situations of joyful mothers, flirtatious maids, and mothers of unwanted children in the park. Pathetically the story concludes, "And you who yearn for a child, who love children, you who would give a part of your own life to hold an infant next to your breast instead of the lap dog . . . to you it is forbidden to give birth. . . . life and joy are forbidden fruit to you. . . . for an indelible mark was cast upon you. . . . you are a spinster." RP Papers.

80. The Hapgood-Pesotta relationship also echoes Anzia Yezierska's romance with John Dewey. As Mary V. Dearborn writes: "She invested John Dewey with all the qualities she felt she lacked, all the avenues that were closed to her, all the possibilities of the promised land." Dearborn, *Love in the Promised Land: The Story of Anzia Yezierska and John Dewey* (New York, 1988).

81. Alice Wexler, *Emma Goldman in America* (Boston, 1984), 138.

82. Wexler, *Emma Goldman*, 158.

83. Emma Goldman to Ben Reitman, 26 July 1911, quoted in Wexler, *Emma Goldman*, 161. Interestingly, Wexler claims that Powers Hapgood's uncle Hutchins was Emma Goldman's "most intimate friend . . . outside of her immediate *Mother Earth* circle." Ibid., 199.

84. Wexler, *Emma Goldman*, 279–80.

85. This desire for the conventional may, in part, explain her marriage to Albert Martin in 1953. Martin, also known as Frank Lopez, shared Pesotta's political beliefs; in fact they first met through the Sacco and Vanzetti Defense Committee. Emotionally, though, they were incompatible, a social butterfly and a drone. The brief marriage ended in divorce. Leeder, *Gentle General*, 152–53.

86. Pesotta was not alone in this assessment. Len De Caux, a labor journalist, remembered her as "one of Dubinsky's best gifts to the CIO." De Caux, *Labor Radical*, 257.

87. In 1944, Pesotta underscored the patriotic tone of the book by signing 300 copies of *Bread upon the Waters* as a gift to the USO. RP Papers, (photos).

88. RP to Powers Hapgood, 5 November 1944, RP Papers.

89. Pesotta, "Life Goes On Amidst the Ruins" (1946), RP Papers.

90. Several times in *Bread upon the Waters*, Pesotta speaks of telling anti-Semites that she is a Jew.

91. Rose Pesotta, "Testimonial," Los Angeles, 27 February 1942, RP Papers.

92. Virginia Yans-McLaughlin, "Metaphors of Self in History: Subjectivity, Oral Narrative, and Immigration Studies," in Virginia Yans-McLaughlin, *Immigration Reconsidered: History, Sociology, and Politics* (New York, 1990), 265.

93. Virginia Yans-McLaughlin, comparing oral interviews of Jewish and Italian women, notes, "Jewish women were less willing than Italians to share their interior worlds with interviewers. . . . their choice of language . . . reveals a comfortable preference for political rhetoric." Yans-McLaughlin, "Metaphors," 282.

94. Histadrut also operated the national health insurance, owned one of the largest banks, and was one of the largest employers in Israel. It was a successor to the Bund and seemed to fit Pesotta's vision of labor organizations. I am indebted to David Katzman for this information.

95. RP to Mollie Steimer, 23 May 1949, RP Papers.

96. RP diaries, 26 November 1949, RP Papers.

97. RP, "They Know What They Want in Israel" (June 1950), RP Papers.

98. Pesotta wrote an account of her trip to Israel entitled "Shalom Chaverim," 11 October 1950, RP Papers. Also of interest is "Histadrut—The Labor Movement in Israel," delivered at the Religion and Labor Conference in Cincinnati, Ohio, 28–30 March 1949.

99. In response to a 1950 Women's Bureau questionnaire entitled "What Are My Reasons for Working?" Pesotta wrote an essay that described the shop. Her papers also contain a photograph taken in 1954 at a celebratory dinner of a graying Pesotta in evening dress with several Black and White women from her shop. RP Papers.

100. Quoted in Leeder, *Gentle General*, 186.

101. RP speech at Atran House, 15 January 1961, RP Papers.

SUGGESTIONS FOR
FURTHER READING

Histories of women's relationship to work, reform, and feminism in the twentieth century are one of the richest veins in the burgeoning field of U.S. women's history. Good general works include Alice Kessler-Harris, *Out to Work: A History of Wage-Earning Women in the United States* (New York, 1982); Rosalind Rosenberg, *Divided Lives: American Women in the Twentieth Century* (New York, 1992); Sara Evans, *Born for Liberty: A History of Women in America* (New York, 1989); Nancy Woloch, *Women and the American Experience* (New York, 1994); and Lynn Weiner, *From Working Girl to Working Mother: The Female Labor Force in the United States, 1820–1980* (Chapel Hill, N.C., 1985). A useful bibliographical essay is Lois Helmbold and Ann Schofield, "Current Trends in Women's Labor History," *Reviews in American History* (December 1989), 501–18.

Useful biographies of woman reformers and labor leaders include: Rosalind Rosenberg, *Beyond Separate Spheres: Intellectual Roots of Modern Feminism* (New Haven, Conn., 1982); Kathryn Kish Sklar, *Florence Kelley and the Nation's Work: The Rise of Women's Political Culture, 1830–1900* (New Haven, Conn., 1995); Diane Kirkby, *Alice Henry: The Power of Pen and Voice: The Life of an Australian-American Labor Reformer* (New York, 1991); Elizabeth Anne Payne, *Reform, Labor, and*

Feminism: Margaret Dreier Robins and the Women's Trade Union League (Urbana, Ill., 1988); Barbara Sicherman, *Alice Hamilton: A Life in Letters* (Cambridge, Mass., 1984); Susan Ware, *Partner and I: Molly Dewson, Feminism, and New Deal Politics* (New Haven, Conn., 1987); Ellen Condliffe Lagemann, *A Generation of Women: Education in the Lives of Progressive Reformers* (Cambridge, Mass., 1979); Ellen Fitzpatrick, *Endless Crusade: Women Social Scientists and Progressive Reform* (New York, 1992); Annelise Orleck, *Common Sense and a Little Fire: Women and Working Class Politics in the United States, 1900–1965* (Chapel Hill, N.C., 1995); Elisabeth I. Perry, *Belle Moskowitz: Feminine Politics and the Exercise of Power in the Age of Alfred E. Smith* (New York, 1987); Lela B. Costin, *Two Sisters for Justice: A Biography of Grace and Edith Abbott* (Champaign-Urbana, Ill., 1983); and Nina Asher, "Dorothy Jacobs Bellanca," in Joan M. Jensen and Sue Davidson, eds., *A Needle, A Bobbin, A Strike: Women Needleworkers in America* (Philadelphia, 1984).

In addition to these biographies, histories of women and labor reform or activism in the early twentieth century include Nancy A. Hewitt and Suzanne Lebsock, eds., *Visible Women: New Essays on American Activism* (Urbana, Ill., 1993); Ruth Milkman, *Women, Work, and Protest: A Century of U.S. Women's Labor History* (Boston, 1985); Robyn Muncy, *Creating a Female Dominion in American Reform, 1890–1935* (New York, 1991); Nancy Schrom Dye, *As Equals and as Sisters: Feminism, Unionism, and the Women's Trade Union League of New York* (Columbia, Mo., 1980); Judith Baer, *The Chains of Protection: The Judicial Response to Women's Labor Legislation* (Westport, Conn., 1978); and Susan Lehrer, *Origins of Protective Labor Legislation for Women, 1905–1925* (Albany, N.Y., 1987). A good introduction to the growing topic of women and the welfare state is Seth Koven and Sonia Michel, eds., *Mothers of a New World: Maternalist Politics and the Origins of Welfare States* (New York, 1993).

Changing aspects of the suffrage movement in the twentieth century have been analyzed by several historians. Ellen Carol DuBois deals with the relationship between working-class and middle-class women in "Working Women, Class Relations, and Suffrage Militance: Harriet Stanton Blatch and the New York Women's Suffrage Movement, 1894–1909," *Journal of American History* 74 (June 1987): 34–58; Mari Jo Buhle describes the links between socialism and suffrage in *Women and American Socialism, 1870–1920* (Champaign-Urbana, Ill., 1981). Sharon Hartman Strom uses a state campaign to study changing strategies in the movement in "Leadership and Tactics in the American Suffrage Movement: A New Perspective from Massachusetts," *Journal of American History* 62 (September 1975): 296–315. The best intellectual history of suffrage remains Aileen Kraditor's *The Ideas of the Woman Suffrage Movement, 1890–1920* (New York, 1971), and the most sophisticated study of feminism in the early twentieth century is Nancy Cott's *The Grounding of Modern Feminism* (New Haven, Conn., 1987). A survey of the tortured history of the Equal Rights Amendment in the United States can be found in Joan Hoff-Wilson, ed., *Rights of Passage: The Past and Future of the ERA* (Bloomington, Ind., 1986).

Histories of women in specific occupations can be found in David Katzman, *Seven Days a Week: Women and Domestic Service in Industrializing America* (New York, 1978); Daniel Sutherland, *Americans and Their Servants: Domestic Service in the United States from 1800 to 1920* (Baton Rouge, 1981); Susan Porter Benson, *Counter Cultures: Saleswomen, Managers, and Customers in American Department Stores, 1890–1940* (Urbana, Ill., 1986); Dorothy Sue Cobble, *Dishing It Out: Waitresses and Their Unions in the Twentieth Century* (Urbana, Ill., 1991); Cindy Aron, *Ladies and Gentlemen of the Civil Service: Middle Class Workers in Victorian America* (New York, 1987); and Angel Kwolek-Folland, *Engendering Business: Men and Women in the Corporate Office, 1870–1930* (Baltimore, 1994).

Women, particularly immigrant women, in the turn-of-the-century city are described in Joanne Meyerowitz, *Women Adrift: Independent Wage Earners in Chicago, 1880–1930* (Chicago, 1988); Kathy Peiss, *Cheap Amusements: Work and Leisure in Turn-of-the-Century New York* (Philadelphia, 1986); Elizabeth Ewen, *Immigrant Women in the Land of Dollars: Life and Culture on the Lower East Side, 1890–1925* (New York, 1985); and Susan A. Glenn, *Daughters of the Shtetl: Life and Labor in the Immigrant Generation* (Ithaca, N.Y., 1990).

INDEX

Page numbers in italics refer to illustrations.